Francis Clemow

Report upon the feasibility and advantages of a waterway

connecting Lake Huron with the St. Lawrence

via the Ottawa River - the Montreal, Ottawa and Georgian Georgian Bay Canal

Francis Clemow

Report upon the feasibility and advantages of a waterway connecting Lake Huron with the St. Lawrence
via the Ottawa River - the Montreal, Ottawa and Georgian Georgian Bay Canal

ISBN/EAN: 9783742858092

Manufactured in Europe, USA, Canada, Australia, Japa

Cover: Foto ©ninafisch / pixelio.de

Manufactured and distributed by brebook publishing software
(www.brebook.com)

Francis Clemow

Report upon the feasibility and advantages of a waterway connecting Lake Huron with the St. Lawrence

APPENDIX No. 4

REPORT, ETC.

OF THE

Special Committee of the Senate of Canada

UPON THE

FEASIBILITY AND ADVANTAGES OF A WATERWAY CONNECTING
LAKE HURON WITH THE ST. LAWRENCE via THE
OTTAWA RIVER—THE MONTREAL, OTTAWA
AND GEORGIAN BAY CANAL.

3RD SESSION, 8TH PARLIAMENT, 61 VICTORIA, 1898

PRINTED BY ORDER OF PARLIAMENT

OTTAWA
PRINTED BY S. E. DAWSON, PRINTER TO THE QUEEN'S MOST
EXCELLENT MAJESTY
1898

REPORT

EVIDENCE and other documents presented to the Senate by the Special
Committee appointed to investigate and report upon the feasibility of,
and the advantages which accrue to the Dominion, from the construction
of a canal uniting the waters of Lake Huron with those of the St.
Lawrence via the Ottawa River— with power to send for papers, persons
and records, and to employ such persons as the Committee may deem
necessary for the investigation, and to report from time to time.

ORDER OF REFERENCE.

EXTRACT FROM THE MINUTES OF PROCEEDINGS OF THE SENATE.

Friday, 18th February, 1898.

The Honourable Mr. Clemow moved, seconded by the Honourable Mr. Casgrain,

That a Select Committee be appointed to investigate and report upon the feasibility of, and the advantages which would accrue to the Dominion from the construction of a canal uniting the waters of Lake Huron with those of the St. Lawrence via the Ottawa River, the said Committee to consist of the Honourable Messieurs Sir Mackenzie Bowell, Scott, Casgrain, McMillan, Dobson, Bellerose, de Boucherville, Ogilvie, Owens, Almon, Miller, McKay, Power, Bernier, Boulton, Perley, Macdonald (P.E.I.), Prowse, Reid, and the mover; with power to send for papers, persons and records, and to employ such persons as the Committee may deem necessary for the purpose of the investigation, and to report from time to time.

The question of concurrence being put thereon, the same was resolved in the affirmative. and

Ordered, accordingly.

REPORT.

THE SENATE,
COMMITTEE ROOM No. 8,
WEDNESDAY, 1st June, 1898.

Your Committee appointed to investigate and report upon the feasibility of, and the advantages which would accrue to the Dominion from the construction of a canal uniting the waters of Lake Huron with those of the St. Lawrence *via* the Ottawa River—with power to send for papers, persons and records, and to employ such persons as the Committee might deem necessary for the investigation and to report from time to time; have the honour to make their final report, as follows:—

Your Committee had before them personally, Mr. S. A. Thompson, of Duluth, whom they have reason to believe, is one of the greatest authorities upon the waterways of America.

Major General Gascoigne, the Commanding Officer of the Canadian Militia.

Mr. Marcus Smith, M. Inst. C. E., of Ottawa.

Mr. James Moldrum, M. Inst. C.E., of London, England, the head of the Foreign Department of Messrs. S. Pearson & Son (Limited), the foremost and most extensive contractors in England, who have been approached with regard to constructing and operating the proposed canal.

Mr. Ormond Higman, Chief Dominion Electrician, Ottawa.

Mr. H. K. Wicksteed, C.E., of Cobourg, who has been over the work and studied it fully.

Your Committee have also received answers to a series of questions sent to various parties, among others—Sir Wm. Van Horne, President of the Canadian Pacific Railway Company ; Mr. Walter Shanly, C.E.; Mr. T. C. Clark, M. Inst. C.E., &c., of New York; Mr. R. W. Shepherd, Man. Dir. of the Ottawa River Navigation Company; Mr. Andrew Bell, C.E., Almonte, and many others.

From an Engineering standpoint, those experts who have traversed the proposed route, and those who have carefully examined the data supplied them, report that no physical difficulty exists in the construction of such a waterway.

Mr. T. C. Clark, M. Inst. C. E., in his report to the Government of Canada, in 1860, says:—

"In the first place I have to report that the distance between Montreal and the mouth of the French River on Lake Huron (according to the plans furnished me by the department), is, following the line of navigation adopted, 430·76 miles.

"That of this distance 351·81 miles are already a perfect natural navigation, and require no improvement, and that it is perfectly practicable so to improve the remaining 78·95 miles, as to convert the whole chain of waters into a first-class navigation for steam vessels, and to reduce the length of canalling to 29·32 miles, or, exclusive of the Lachine Canal, to 20·82 miles."

They also desire to call attention to the advantage to be derived therefrom, as respects the present settlers of the North-west; as also to the impetus that would ensue in the future to the increase of the agricultural population of that fertile section of the country by affording them easy, cheap and safe transportation for their products, and thus the large area of land now unproductive, would become owned by a desirable producing class of settlers, who would consequently be contributors to the revenue of the Dominion. Under the various circumstances, your Committee would strongly recommend the contemplated enterprise to the favourable consideration of the Government, and that they may be pleased to extend such assistance in such manner, mode and conditions as will ensure the early construction and speedy completion of the work; feeling quite assured that the people of the Country when they are made aware of the advantages to be derived from the undertaking, will duly appreciate any action the Government may take which will facilitate the construction of a work of such National importance; it being an all-Canadian route from and to the seaboard to the North-west.

Your Committee deeming that the information now embraced in their Report, with the Evidence of the various persons, now presented, should be circulated as extensively as possible; would recommend that five thousand copies in English and two thousand copies in French, with Maps and profiles (in addition to the regular distribution number), be printed as soon as possible for general distribution.

All which is respectfully submitted.

FRANCIS CLEMOW,
Chairman.

MINUTES OF EVIDENCE.

THE SENATE,
OTTAWA, 23rd March, 1898.

The Committee met at 11.30 a.m.

Mr. S. A. THOMPSON, of Duluth, appeared and addressed the Committee as follows:—

Mr. Chairman and Gentlemen of this Honourable Committee: I understand it to be the wish of Mr. McLeod Stewart that I should proceed to make a statement rather than that he should bring out the points which I have to present to you by question and answer. Of course it goes without saying that it is the privilege of this Honourable Committee, and my desire quite as well, if there be anything in my testimony that you wish to ask questions about, that I am certainly at your disposition. Not knowing exactly the amount of time which you can allow me, I shall endeavour to go as rapidly as I may to lay for your consideration the broad basis, first of the value of waterway improvements in general, second of their importance to a community, and third of their importance in promoting certain interests which ordinarily—at least, that is on the other side of the line—are considered somewhat antagonistic. I must take a moment to express my great pleasure at the honour which has been conferred upon me to be called before this Honourable Committee of our neighbour sister nation here upon the north, to speak upon a subject which has been near my heart for many years. I am called in my own country—and I glory in the title—a crank on the subject of waterway improvements, but I believe I can give good grounds for the faith that is in me, and I hope to present to you, not perhaps many new facts, but as is often the case, to throw a side light on them which will aid you in your deliberations on the matter before you. A certain distinguished ex-Governor of the State of New York once remarked that economy of transportation of persons and property is the chief factor in our modern civilization; it constitutes the marked difference between civilization and barbarism. Doubtless some of you, as I have, have been in Countries where there were no roads. Cutting my way painfully step by step through the jungles of South America, I have understood something about the difference between civilization and barbarism in the matter of transportation. Therefore, if this statement be true, it behooves us to find what is the cheapest form of transportation. Some fifteen years ago two distinguished Railway Presidents, one of them President of an eastern railway, the other President of a western railway, sat talking in an eastern office. The eastern man called attention to the constantly increasing efficiency of railways—the substitution of steel rails for iron, of steel in bridges, of more powerful locomotives, of cars with greater carrying capacity, of the improvements in the way of grades and curves which had been made, so that the roads were carrying very much greater quantities of freight with the same engine and in the same cars and with a much greater degree of economy, and he said, "Canal boats are played out already; the river steamer is almost gone, and it will only be a little while until the steamship of the Great Lakes will follow these others into retirement and leave to the railways the undisputed carrying trade of all the Continent, if not of the world, except on the Ocean where the railways cannot run." The other railway man, telling the story in my hearing a few years ago, said, "I might have continued to believe, as I did then, in the ultimate triumph of the railway if I had not during that time had occasion to operate some steamboats myself." But before I finish the story let me give you just a few points on this subject. I have here, and can give you entire, if you wish, a table compiled from the reports of the Chicago Board of Trade, showing the charges for carrying wheat from Chicago to New York city by three different methods for a series of years—by rail, by lake and rail (that is by lake to Buffalo and thence by rail to New York), and lake, Erie Canal and the Hudson River, the all water route.

Calendar Years.	Lake and canal.	Lake and rail.	All rail.
1868	25·3	29·0	42·6
1869	24·1	25·0	35·1
1870	17·5	22·5	33·3
1871	21·6	35·0	31·0
1872	26·6	28·0	33·5
1873	19·2	26·9	33·2
1874	14·2	16·9	28·7
1875	11·4	14·6	24·1
1876	9·7	11·8	16·5
1877	7·5	15·8	20·3
1878	10·1	11·4	17·7
1879	13·0	13·3	17·3
1880	13·2	15·7	19·7
1881	8·6	10·4	14·4
1882	8·7	10·9	14·6
1883	8·40	11·5	16·5
1884	6·59	9·09	13·2
1885	4·55	9·6	14·0

Since 1885 there have been no radical or marked changes. We find that the all rail rate had decreased to fourteen cents a bushel, while the all water rate had decreased to 4·55 cents per bushel. In other words, while there had been a reduction of two-thirds in the all rail rates, there had been a reduction of 4·5 in the all water rate. So we find during this time the all water has been below the rail rate by from 25 to 67·5 per cent. Now, suppose we take for a moment the cost of transportation: we find that according to Poor's Manual for 1896, the last year for which I have statistics to compare, in 1896 the average rate received by the railways of the United States (and of course you will pardon me for quoting the statistics of my own country, with which I am naturally most familiar) the rate received per ton per mile for the transportation of freight averaged 8·21 mills. There has been a magnificent reduction in the rail rates corresponding to this table which I have shown you here, but suppose we turn now to the water rates. We find that on the Erie Canal the rate is very much less. Turn to the lakes. There at the outlet of Lake Superior the records are kept very close, and in 1896 the average price received for the transportation of freight which went through the canals at the outlet of Lake Superior was ninety-one hundredths of one mill. We can state the fact broadly by saying that in general the cost of deep water transportation is only about one-tenth the average cost of rail transportation. Suppose I go, just for a moment, into a little further elaboration of the figures. During that same year, according to a statement made before a meeting of the Lake Carriers' Association, the average rate of freight transportation on all the Great Lakes was only eighty-five one-hundredths of a mill, and that mainly because there was deeper water in some of the channels below than in the St. Mary's Canal and some of the outlets in that neighbourhood. Let us now find the ultimate limits of competition in order to discover the cheapest known form of transportation. A careful series of experiments conducted on the Grand Trunk Railway here in Canada some years ago showed that the actual net cost of transportation, that is exclusive of interest on bonds, &c., was five mills per ton per mile. The average net cost in 1896 on the railroads of the United States was somewhat larger than that, being nearly six mills per ton per mile. There are a few coal roads where practically all the loads are carried by gravity, and the engines are used merely for the purpose of running the empty cars back again, and on these the average cost is three and a half mills per ton; but the best rate in actual railroad transportation under ordinary conditions is four mills per ton per mile.

Sir MACKENZIE BOWELL—Does that include the long and the short haul?

Mr. THOMPSON—Yes. The road on which freight is carried at that low cost is the Lake Shore and Michigan Southern Railway. Coming back to the story I was starting to tell you about the two railway Presidents, I may mention the name of one of them: the western man was Mr. James Hill, President of the Great Northern Road. He said: "I have built some steamships myself. Those steamships are built to the full draught of water at the Sault." This was before the larger canals were open. "They carry twenty-seven hundred tons of freight, and they make the run from Duluth to Buffalo in three and a half days, and cost an average of $120 per day." Now, in round numbers, almost as exactly as we can name it, the distance from Duluth to Buffalo is 1,000 miles, and working that down we find that the cost is fifteen one thousandths of a cent per ton per mile. Turning that into figures that business men understand better than they can understand these microscopic rates, it means one-twenty-seventh of four mills, and that is the absolute net cost of carrying freight on the Great Lakes. That is to say, we do on the Great Lakes for $1 what it costs the best situated railway in the United States $27 to do. Therefore, without going further into these figures—I could give them by the hour, if necessary—you will agree with me in my conclusion that water transportation is the cheapest, and therefore if economy in transportation is the chief factor in the prosperity of nations, that nation which enlarges its waterways and developes them to the greatest possible extent will have done for its citizens, its producers and its consumers alike, the very best which can be done. But we are not through with these interesting matters. I find on the other side of the line that there has been some times a question in the minds of some of us whether the people run the railroads or the railroads run the people. I do not know, of course, whether you have any such questions over here; I merely wish to point out the fact that we have found, and we have the testimony of most eminent railway men, Mr. Albert Fink, who was Railway Commissioner, Mr. G. R. Blanchard, one of the most noted railway men in the country—they all testify, and without going into it at length, I will sum up their conclusion—that water competition is the most powerful possible regulator of railway rates which can be conceived, far exceeding in its power and operation any of the edicts of legislative bodies, even though they be the highest in the land. For instance, Mr. Fink points out that a few sailing vessels at Chicago, in connection with a few canal boats on the Erie Canal, have been able, during the season of navigation, to fix the rates for the transportation of grain from Chicago to New York. Does it stop there? No. Here are the Lake Shore and the New York Central which practically form a continuous line which parallels the waterway from Chicago to New York, they are compelled to make their rates under stress of water competition. Competing roads cannot impose higher rates than those which prevail on the Lake Shore and Michigan Central and New York Central; if they do, the business goes to the New York Central. So you follow it on to lines further south, the Baltimore and Ohio, the Louisville and Nashville, down to the Gulf of Mexico. Their rates are fixed, or materially modified during the season of navigation by the competition of a few sailing boats on the Great Lakes and a few canal boats on the Erie Canal. When I have talked for a time about the cheapness of water transportation as compared with rail transportation, and urged that we should have the waterway improvements made in order that we might get for the people of the country cheaper transportation, since they made the most tremendously powerful regulator of railway rates possible, I have been asked, "Well, but do you want to drive all the railways into bankruptcy?" Not at all, gentlemen, and let me make to you what will appear at first sight, a paradoxical statement, and then proceed to prove it, not by any opinions of mine, but by the uncontrovertible logic of facts that you cannot dispute, that waterway improvements not only promote the prosperity of the people in general, but that the best thing that could happen to every railway in the world would be to have a waterway at least twenty-one feet deep parallel to every mile of its track. And I will say, to bring the thing out broadly and flatly, to bring it right down to the case that is being considered in this honourable committee, that the railroads that run from Ottawa to Lake Huron and the Georgian Bay would be doing the best possible thing for themselves and their stockholders and the dividends they are able to pay, if they would underwrite the bonds of this canal along the Ottawa River, and see that it is built as soon as men and money could achieve it. Does that seem ridiculous ? Do you smile at it ? Give me fifteen minutes and I will do the smiling, with the honourable gentlemen's permission. The best thing always to do is simply to go to the facts. I do not happen to have a newspaper in my pocket, but it makes no difference about that. I make the broad statement and you can verify it any day you please. Take up the stock quotations, and take the railroads like the New York Central and the roads running alongside of waterways generally, and you will find their stock quoted higher every day in the year than the roads away off inland that do not touch water except when they stop at the tanks for the engine to take water. There is my first point, and I know that it is so. The stock of the New York Central and roads alongside of great waterways is higher because it is worth more, because the traffic is there and the dividend is earned. But let us go a little further. I am sorry that the rapidity with which I came from the sunny groves of Florida to the capital of the Dominion did not give me time to go to my home where I had a great mass of papers which I must now quote to you, but if there be any gentleman who doubts the accuracy of the figures I give, I can send him the official documents later. I have on file a letter from President Ingalls of the Chesapeake and Ohio road. President Ingalls was fearful at one time when the Government of the United States took up the improvements of the Great Kanawha River that it might interfere with the traffic on his road. But what is the fact ? The traffic of the river increased, of course ; they took out bars and put in locks and dams and opened up the river for good sized boats, where formerly one-half of the year it was dried up and the other half frozen up. The traffic of the river increased tremendously. President Ingalls writes me, sends me a statement, that the traffic on his road, not merely the general traffic, but the traffic in coal originating on the Great Kanawha River has increased in great proportions, and we have no warmer friend of waterway improvement in the United States than President Ingalls of the Chesapeake and Ohio road. I have a letter from Chauncy M. Depew, the President of the New York Central, in which he says that as the result of years of study in the matter that anything that would damage the Erie Canal and its efficiency would damage his road, that he is in favour of every improvement to increase its efficiency, knowing it increases the traffic of his road. I will give the Committee the reasons in a little while, but let me give you the absolute facts just now. A few years ago they canalized the River Main from Frankfort to Mayence. The first year after that improvement was completed the business of the river increased sixty-four per cent, and the next year it made a further increase of thirty-six per cent. There is a railroad right along each bank of that river between those same places. These roads had been in trouble for years. For a time the cities had nothing to sell and everything to buy. The trains went loaded one way and empty the other. Did these roads go on down into hopeless bankruptcy ? Not at all. The very first year after the improvements were completed, coincident with that enormous increase of traffic on the river of which I have spoken, the traffic of the roads increased thirty-eight per cent; and the second year the traffic increased fifty-six per cent more. They went with loaded trains in both directions and paid dividends for the first time in a good many years. Let me proceed. I can give you these statistics for a long time, but I do not wish to tire the patience of the Committee completely. Take France. France began building canals one hundred years before Christ and has never stopped since. Wars and revolutions have taken place, and they have simply hindered or delayed for a little time. But through the very wars and the terrible upheavals that have come to that country, they have kept on building canals until to-day, they have eight thousand miles of canals and improved rivers in that country.

And as I have sometimes said on our side of the line, take our state of Texas and convert it into a circular sea, and convert France into a circular island, and there would be a strip of sea one hundred miles wide around the island, and yet that little country since 1814—go no farther back than that—has spent upon water improvements seven hundred and fifty million dollars, and has spent seven hundred millions on railways, and about six hundred and fifty million dollars on their wagon roads. And while for a time it was a mystery to me, the way in which France paid off her war indemnity after the war with Germany, I am convinced now, that the fundamental reason is, that she has a system of transportation, railways, wagon roads and waterways, a trinity of transportation which is equalled by no other country in the world. Transportation is a tax. When you make transportation the least bit higher than it should be, it constitutes an unnecessary tax. If by some magic we could bring the grain from your western prairies here to your consumers, the farmer would get more and the consumer would pay less than is the case now. However, here is a special point I wanted to call your attention to in speaking of France. They have over there a system of Government guarantees of railway earnings, that their earnings will not be less than a certain amount, and we find that in the districts where they have the greatest canal traffic there they also have the greatest railway traffic. To name one specific instance, the Great Northern Railway of France traverses a district in which there is fifty three per cent of the total boating capacity of France, and that railway is the only one in the country—speaking of a few years ago—which was not obliged to call upon the Government to make good its guarantee. Take another notable instance. I have so many here that I find it is going to take too long. Let me give you one further and notable instance. During the time the Elbe River in Bohemia was being improved—fifteen years was the time—the steamboat traffic, the river traffic, quintupled: it was five times as great at the end of the fifteen years when the improvements were finished as it was at the beginning. During that time the traffic of the railroads running alongside that river increased still more largely, and the dividend on the main line of the road rose to sixteen per cent per annum. I will quote one more instance, and this will be the last of the figures which I will inflict upon you. Germany in 1888 ordered the construction of 1,000 miles more of canal, and the improvement of about 500 miles more of river, although she had at that time 1,300 miles of canal and 5,000 miles of improved navigable rivers already. Now consider that at the same date out of a total of 16,281 miles of railway in Germany, 14,665 belonged to and were operated by the government. Does anybody think the government of Germany was foolish enough to spend these millions of marks upon the improvement of waterways if the result was going to be to decrease the revenue of the Government upon their railways? Not at all. They simply were working according to the result of years of observation, whereby they know that the improvement of the waterway is the surest way, not only to promote the prosperity of the country, but to increase the dividend of the railways that paralleled those waterways. I think perhaps I have gone on that line far enough, unless some gentleman has a question that he wishes to ask. I will state now in a very few words why this takes place, what the fundamental and underlying reason is. It is this: an analysis of the traffic at the Sault Canals shows, that the great bulk of the material transported on waterways is raw materials. It is iron ore, it is grain, it is lumber, it is stone, things in which the weight and tonnage is very large in proportion to the value. The Great Western Railway of England conducted an investigation some time ago. They got into the habit over there of doing just what some railroad men did in the United States, straining every nerve to drive the canals totally out of business, and they wondered why, with all the business they were doing, they did not have more dividend, and they found that the manager, acting under a mistaken idea, was using fifty-eight per cent of their equipment, in a traffic which produced only fourteen per cent of their revenue. They were killing the goose that laid the golden egg. Take the River Main, from Frankfort to Mayence. The opening up of navigation led them to open up the coal mines, and so on, and it produced a different traffic, and increased the business of the railroad. When the elevated railroads were asking for a franchise in New York, the surface roads, the horse car lines, were afraid that if they got that thing up there in the air they would have to go into bankruptcy. Has it proven so? Not at all. The elevated roads take the long distance traffic, leaving to the horse car lines the short distance traffic, and also the benefit of the growth which came from the development caused by the fact that it was possible to come down on the elevated train. So that to-day, with the elevated roads paying large dividends, carrying an enormous number of passengers, having developed a traffic which it was impossible for the surface roads to take care of, the surface roads are paying greater dividends than ever before, and are at great expense changing their lines into electric and cable lines, in order to go faster and take care of the business crowding upon them. In other words when you develop a waterway, you make possible the carrying, in the cheapest possible form, of raw material. When you take manufactured goods, from silks and jewellery down to things which are of a lower grade, comparatively few people can tranship a million dollars' worth of goods of that kind. But, gentlemen, when you get millions of tons of raw materials, it needs a metropolis to handle them, and it produces a metropolis in the manufacture of them. I have gone over the matter rather rapidly, I admit, not desiring to trespass upon your time, and leave to the gentlemen of the Committee to ask any specific questions they may wish to put to me, to point out to you these great fundamental facts. Just for a moment let me speak of this canal. I will say that the very first time that my attention was called to this matter was by Mr. A. M. Wellington, now deceased, at that time one of the editors of the *Engineering News* of New York, and universally recognized among us as one of the greatest Engineers of his day. I have been, as any of these gentlemen who may possibly have heard of me at waterway conventions anywhere will know, I have been for a great many years an enthusiastic advocate of a ship canal out from the lakes to the sea, and naturally I have urged that it be built in our own territory, and I have too high an idea of gentlemen who are British subjects to understand they would expect me to be otherwise than a loyal American, to look after the interests of my country honourably, as you look after yours. And I said to Mr. Wellington: "yes, I think we ought to have a canal, and it should go from Niagara Falls and down the Hudson and so on." And Mr. Wellington brought down from his desk a map, and he showed me the wonderful line up from the Hudson to the St. Lawrence, across to the Ottawa, up the Ottawa and Lake Nipissing, and into Georgian Bay. He called my attention to it, and I wonder gentlemen if it has ever been called to your attention just in that way—the most marvellous approach to an air line of inland water transportation in the world, from the head of Lake Superior to tide water in Montreal. And he said: "We can get thirty feet of water up the Ottawa route, enough to accommodate the largest ocean vessel that floats, for half what it will cost to put it in any other way into the great lakes," and that is what called my attention first to this marvellous approach to an air line; to the natural conditions, so much of the way lying through rock which is solid enough that when you have blasted out the place for your lock you have only to put a little bit of cement on the side to cover up the rough places, and it makes a lock chamber which will be strong enough and staunch enough to stand till the end of time; to the wonderful long reaches where it is deep already, naturally going along the quiet waters, and then rapids and falls concentrated close together, so that it is an easy matter to put the locks in there which will let them down into the next level, and so they go. And as far as the water supplies are concerned, we know how it takes its origin up there among the lakes and the forests, and how very little variation there is, how you can count on a certain supply of water from year's end to year's end, and vessels know how deep they may load without striking the bottom. And then the character of the country—it would be superfluous for me to talk to you about it—its resources, minerals and lumber, and so on. And I must say a word about another matter. Some people thought canals were done with, and we find they were mistaken. For a long time people thought that the water powers were practically gone out, that the steam engine was going to make them of no account, but the developments that have been brought about by Edison and still more by that modern wizard Nicola Tesla, have made a new era for water power. As I have travelled on the railroad which runs up the Ottawa Valley and watched from the windows of the car the great water powers on the Ottawa, not to say anything of your magnificent water power here, I thought of the power which you can develop by the construction of this canal, which will be not only a waterway for vessels; but, a magnificent source of water power every few miles; of the electrical distribution which can make it in large units or small units; that you can utilize it at the side of the water power or 100 miles away, you can make this beautiful Ottawa Valley one of the great manufacturing districts of the world from end to end. It is not at all impossible that the Canadian Pacific Railway—I speak of this railway because for a considerable distance it runs along side the Ottawa River—may run its trains from Montreal to Winnipeg by water-power. You know that trains are run on the New York and Hartford Railway by electricity and they are using electric power to take trains on the Baltimore and Ohio Railway through tunnels at Baltimore. The day of electricity for railway purposes is coming and when you have the unlimited power of water, renewed, as certain as the promise of God holds sure that summer and winter and rain and sunshine shall follow in succession, when you have the water powers and the genius of men to furnish dynamos to convert them into electricity, we shall ride on the railroads and not get cinders in our eyes because there will not be any cinders there. I have already given you figures to show the economy of water transportation. The thought just occurs to me that it will cheapen not only the business already in existence, but business yet to be developed. Take this official statement here of the tonnage through the canals at the Sault, and this by the courtesy of the officials in charge of the Canadian canals includes the traffic through your Canadian canals also, so we have the total traffic of Lake Superior. How it has grown! Go back to 1855 when that canal was opened; there went through that year a total registered tonnage of vessels of 106,296 tons. During the year 1897 there went through the canals at the outlet of Lake Superior—and, gentlemen, you and I, Canadians and Americans alike, can be proud of the fact that there is such an enormous traffic away in the heart of the continent—the traffic has been enormous. The two governments have built three ship locks and any one of the three is larger than any other to be found elsewhere in the world, except the two that lie close alongside of it. Through these three magnificent locks there passed last year 18,982,755 tons of freight. Back in 1852, when they were considering the question in Congress of giving a land grant to the State of Michigan to build these first little locks at the Sault, Henry Clay rose in Congress and said: "The thing is as wild as a proposition to build a railroad to the moon." In 1853, after the land grant had been turned over to the state of Michigan and the legislature of the state was considering what size of a lock should be built, Mr. E.B. Ward, of Detroit, who is recognized even at this day as one of the most far-sighted business men ever connected with the trade on the lakes, wrote to a friend in the Legislature that "by advocating locks of such enormous size, locks which will not be needed for a century, if ever, you are jeopardizing the success of the whole project." The little locks were completed and the canal was opened in 1855. Did they solve the problem? No; as you know, in 1881 our government supplemented them with another lock 513 feet long, 85 feet wide and 17 feet deep on the sill. Now, the Engineers said, and I have had many a talk with Gen. Poe since, "We have solved the problem of a connection between Lake Superior and the other lakes for all time to come." The year in which that lock was opened had not expired before they saw that the trade had outgrown that lock. They have blown out the little locks and put in a lock 800 feet long, and 21 feet deep on the mitre sill; and you in Canada have put in a larger lock on your side, and Gen. Poe, sitting on the shore and looking at the great vessels coming in to be locked through, said: "I am an old man now," touching his gray hairs, "but if you live out your days you will see this magnificent lock of 1881, which, until the Canadian lock was completed a few months ago, was the finest in the world, blown out with dynamite as the little lock of 1855 was, and another put in with not less than twenty-six feet, perhaps thirty feet on the mitre sill. I have watched this traffic for thirty years and no man has been able to keep up with its growth, for the wildest dream of one year seems tame beside the reality of the next." Here is a little hint of the magnificent country that lies beyond; I know something of my own country, Minnesota, (my home State), Iowa, Dakota, and those States which sweep westward to the Pacific. I have also had the pleasure of knowing something by personal observation of your Canadian North-west and it was my good fortune to enlighten James G. Blaine as to the character of that region. We Americans thought he was pretty well informed on most topics, but he had read and believed that article which I cannot think of without laughing, published by C. Wood Davis in a magazine, in which he said that the United States would soon be a wheat importing rather than a wheat exporting country, but this is the particular remark which I laughed at—he said, "The whole of the country north of the international boundary line adapted to the cultivation of wheat is so small that it may be left out of consideration." (Laughter). While I was travelling for days in that country, by the courtesy of some of your officials, I was taken in charge by that most admirable organization, the Mounted Police, and went away out beyond the railroad—went up and down, and back and forth, and had the honour to be upon the train for some days in which their Excellencies the Governor General and Lady Aberdeen were making a visit to the North-west, and I saw away up yonder on the North Saskatchewan, where the average American thinks the ice is always at least 10 feet thick, (laughter)—I saw a watermelon which had been grown there, weighing seventy-four pounds. That was in October. I had read something about that country. I count among my friends Consul Taylor, whom the people of Winnipeg knew and loved, who through all the changes of our administrations for twenty-one years represented the United States there, and was loved, if possible, more by the Canadians than by the Americans (applause)—I had read his reports and knew something of the resources and possibilities of that country, but I went to what was considered the jumping off place and found that they had incandescent lights in the hotel where I stopped, and they brought in plates to dinner that I was obliged to drop when I touched, because they were so hot, something you could not have got so far west on our own side of the line. It was the sixteenth day of October, yet they had on the table two dishes of ripe tomatoes which had been raised in that locality out of doors. I have learned something by personal observation of Manitoba, Assiniboia, Alberta and British Columbia, and by reading of things that lie still further beyond. I have talked with men representing your own Government who have gone on beyond where I have been, and from reading the reports they have given, I say to you: gentlemen, the day is coming, and it is not very far in the century that is about to dawn, when the Canadian North-west is going to regulate the wheat and flour market of the world (applause). When I have stood in conventions, meeting my good friends—and I am glad to say I have many on the Canadian side—and have advocated that my own government should build a ship canal through our own territory from the lakes to the sea, I have said I am just as willing to go, as I now have the honour of doing, to plead with your government to build another ship canal through your territory. And further, when you go by the Ottawa route and we go out by Oswego, is that going to be all? No; take the St. Lawrence, too, and I say to you, gentlemen, and I repeat it in all honesty, that the man who does not understand that all three of those routes are going to be needed, and every inch of water that can be got in them to transport the magnificent products of the combined Canadian and United States North-west, has not realized the magnificent endowment of this continent. I have sometimes thought that the Great Index shaped finger at the west end of Lake Superior, was put there by the Almighty to point to the final seat of power upon the earth. I say it without any political meaning, "what God has joined together, no man can put asunder, and we Anglo-Saxons, while under different flags, over all is the Cross of the Christian religion that we both profess, and I believe it to be that God has put into this great North America the point where the Anglo-Saxon race shall have the seat of its power to dominate the earth, not for universal conquest, but to compel universal peace. So I have travelled over your land, I have gone up and down your Ottawa, I have gone over the length and breadth of the lakes, your lakes as well as ours, and I have studied this matter of transportation until again I say to you, as Gentlemen representing this great Dominion and legislating for its advancement, nothing can so advance it as to increase the means of transportation. You have done grandly already. You have done infinitely better in proportion to your population and resources than our country has done, but do not be weary of well-doing. Open your St. Lawrence canals. We in the Western States are waiting and praying for the day when ships can go through from Montreal to Duluth without breaking bulk. It means value to us, and it means business for you. Open those other marvellous waterways. It is not for me to say just how deep your Ottawa Canal should be, but I say to you that for every foot less than twenty-six feet in depth, you build it in the first place, there will be increased cost and increased work for you in the future. Build it as deep as you can now, and let the traffic that is to come provide for its enlargement. Let us hope for the day when Ocean steamships will be able to go as freely from the seaboard to the Upper Lakes, as they can pass between Liverpool and New York to-day, and so for the prosperity of your own people, develop this waterway and all your waterways just as fast as your resources will allow it.

Hon. Mr. BERNIER—Have you ever considered the possibility of having a waterway from Winnipeg to Lake Superior ?

Mr. THOMPSON—I believe there is a magnificent possibility, and if the Gentleman will allow me to defer that subject for a moment it will come in appropriately in connection with another matter. The report which your Honourable Chairman holds in his hand shows that of the total traffic out of Lake Superior last year, 19,000,000 tons in round numbers, over 10,000,000 tons was iron ore, and counting the ore which went by rail to Lake Michigan ports there were twelve and a half million tons of iron ore sent out from the Lake Superior region last year. Knowing the cost of transportation in proportion to the value of the product, I am as certain as that I am alive to-day that if, instead of having the Great Lakes to carry out this ore, there had only been broken land or little rivers merely for water and drainage, not one ton of that ore would have been moved. There are over $260,000,000 invested in the mining and transportation of iron ore in the Lake Superior district alone. There would not have been a dollar of that invested if it had not been for the Lakes ; the Lakes make it possible to develop a class of traffic which the railways could not touch. It leaves for the railways the higher class of freight and the passenger traffic. I have sometimes wondered whether the railway men in our country have profited by the lesson which the government in Hungary has furnished by the adoption of the zone system in passenger traffic. After the Government took possession of the railways they marked out certain zones of territory within which certain passenger rates should prevail. The average reduction of rates below those which had been charged under the private ownership of those railways was 82 per cent. What was the result of that reduction ? In seven months the traffic increased one hundred and sixty-nine per cent; the receipts increased 18 per cent, and as the expenses did not increase at all those profits went to dividends. With all due respect to the honourable railroad men of the continent of America, I do not believe that they yet know the tremendous increase in traffic, and consequent increase in net revenue to themselves that comes from diminished cost of transportation. If you can force this matter on their attention by decreasing the cost of transportaton on raw materials like iron ore, lumber and so on, they will find that even without decreasing their rates they will have increased traffic. You will have helped them and helped the country. It is a well known fact that density of traffic enables the companies to decrease their charges, and where you have millions of people to draw on, as, for instance, between New York and Philadelphia, you can make your passenger rate so much per mile and have a profit where you could not cover expenses in a sparsely settled country such as, for instance, the Saskatchewan. You cannot move Manitoba or Assiniboia any nearer to the sea-board, but when you have opened the way for an ocean ship to go up to Lake Superior you have, for all practical purposes, put those great regions a thousand miles nearer the Markets of the World. Not mileage, but cost of transportation is the true commercial measure of distance.

4—2

For the prosperity of your own people, for the development of your resources, for making conditions which will bring millions of population into your fertile lands of the North-west, for the benefit of your railways, improve the waterways. I now come to the question which the Honourable Gentleman (Mr. Bernier) gave me : I have considered it and I fully believe that the time will come when Lake Superior and the Mississippi River will be connected with the 5,000 miles of navigation, with your great Lake Winnipeg, second only to the other great lakes that we have been considering, your Saskatchewan and the Lake of the Woods and all that wonderful waterway in the North-west, over almost every mile of which I have had the pleasure of travelling in canoe and steamboat. And my confidence has been vastly increased by the one final thing which I will mention except to respond to any question which any of you gentlemen may ask. There has been of late an invention which will do as much for Inland navigation as the Locomotive did for land transportation. It was about the time that Columbus was discovering America that the canal lock was invented, and there have been few improvements made in it since. There have been some. In England and at Fontinettes in France, and one or two other places, there are what they called balanced hydraulic lifts. The one at Fontinettes is to overcome a height of fifty-three feet eight inches. That is over near the line between Belgium and France. Where formerly they had five locks and took three-quarters of an hour or more to make the passage from top to bottom or bottom to top, they now have this one balanced hydraulic lock, and they make the total change—hauling in, changing level, and hauling out—in fifteen minutes. The actual change in position is made in seven minutes. That is a grand improvement and reduces the cost very materially. But the invention to which I wish to refer is the Pneumatic lock.

Hon. Mr. DeBoucherville—Are they not trying the same plan on the Erie Canal ?

Mr. Thompson.—No, it is the Pneumatic lock which I am about to describe. Every one has seen the gasometers in which the gas companies store their gas. Suppose we take two immense gasometers and on top of each build a tank to hold water. Of course in this case our gasometers will be built with square corners and our tanks will have gates at each end for the entrance and exit of vessels. Underneath you put a tube connecting one with the other and there is the whole invention. The marvel of it is that no one thought of it before, because the pneumatic caisson has been used in bridge building for years. One gasometer of course is up and the other down. You run in your vessel at the top or at the bottom as the case may be, or one at each end if you choose ; you let in a few inches of water in the top one for the purpose of turning the balance, and open the valve, and the excess of water in one causes it to descend slowly and the other to move slowly up. That is the whole process. Mr. Dutton, the inventor, tells me that he has no doubt he can make a change of one hundred and fifty feet in fifteen minutes. That can be done too so that the cost of the two locks, instead of a great flight of magnificent locks that would be needed by the common method of lockage, will be much less. The main thing is the saving of time, for time is money nowadays in transportation as in everything else. Instead of taking nearly twenty-six hours, as it does now, to pass a vessel through the Welland Canal, Mr. Dutton declares that we can make a canal which will let a boat pass through with just as much safety from Lake Erie down to Lake Ontario, around that magnificent cataract, in two hours time and at one-third of the cost of locking through the ordinary locks. We have a difference in elevation between Lake Superior and Lake of the Woods of about eight hundred feet in all to over-come. Under the ordinary system of locks that would be very expensive. Under the new system, which seeks to mass the lockage all in one place instead of distribut-ing it over a considerable length of canal for the conservation of the water supply, there would be both cheapness and speed, the lockage being concentrated in a few miles by this invention of Mr. Dutton's, which, as the gentleman has just now said, is being tried now on the Erie Canal at Lockport a few miles from Tonawanda. If that experiment should prove successful there, as I have no doubt it will, it will be applied to the whole length of the Erie Canal attaining the minimum of expense with the maximum of efficiency. We will yet bring all the waters of the whole Canadian North-west in connection with the Lakes and through the Lakes with the sea. Here are two small points that I will mention : the crucial point in all Ship canals is the supply of water on the summit level. In the first place when you get to your magnificent locks at the Sault you cannot let a fisherman's boat through without emptying the whole lock of water. Of course there you have the entire body of Lake Superior to draw from. But suppose you were running a vessel through a canal where the water is scarce, the lockmaster would hate to empty a large lock of water for the purpose of passing a small vessel through, but under this system the only water that is wasted is the few inches of water that is let in to overcome the friction. On all canals the traffic conveyed from the less settled part to the densely settled parts of the country is composed of raw materials, so you have a greater tonnage in weight down hill, although the tonnage the other way is of greater value, but in weight the traffic would be three times as much going down hill as the traffic going up hill. That is clearly shown by the Statistics of the traffic from the upper lakes. Now what would be the result under this new system? For every ton that would go up Westward there would be three tons coming down Eastward. Now suppose a vessel enters the upper lock chamber, and there is none to come up. Say it displaces 5,000 tons of water. Now, except for the few inches of water put in to overcome the friction, one lock chamber has taken up 5,000 tons of water more than the other took down, so the ordinary working of the system will be to carry water up to the summit level, and the whole bugaboo of scarcity of water disappears. I am not a mere visionary when I say, that if I live out my days I hope to be able to go not only from my home in the city of Duluth to London in a palace car *via* the Klondike, but in a palace steamer by the Ottawa River, and that we can bring down wheat from all that country, water borne, and the coal which is one hundred and forty-nine feet thick, not perhaps all in one layer, in the Crow's Nest Pass. I saw millions and millions of acres of coal up there running from low grade lignite to the best anthracite, and that will yet be carried in all directions by water transportation. Of course you will have your great Railways, you people who belong to the great British branch of our race know ten times as much about building good roads as we know in the United States—you will have your railway transportation, your waterways, and your wagon ways developed to the highest point, and then you will find prosperity and your power will go beyond the highest dreams of the present time. And the millions will come in there, and for all of them there will be prosperity, and with all the nations of the earth peace.

Hon. Sir MACKENZIE BOWELL.—It has been stated—it is not necessary to mention the name—that you could not find water enough. But I thought that Mr. Thompson answered that point effectively.

Mr. THOMPSON.—With that new system of lockage you get all the water you require. I was asked if I had been over the route in regard to the water supply. I have not been over it in an engineering sense of studying the water supply, but personally I am willing to base my own judgment—until displaced by something better—upon that of Mr. Wellington. He was one of our noted engineers. He had studied this route and he said to me : " The water supply is ample : the other conditions are phenomenal. The finest place upon the globe for a deep ship canal is the Ottawa River route."

Mr. McLEOD STEWART.—I have had a letter from Mr. Wellington to that effect.

The Committee then adjourned.

THE SENATE,
OTTAWA, 3rd May, 1898.

COMMITTEE met this day.

The Honourable MR. CLEMOW, Chairman.

MAJOR GENERAL GASCOIGNE called and examined.

Mr. STEWART—Will you explain the Military advantages of this route?

MAJOR GENERAL GASCOIGNE—I may state broadly, from a strategic point of view, I look upon this scheme as the most desirable possible. Of course, I should qualify my statements in this respect, that a great deal depends upon the depth of the water that you propose to make.

The CHAIRMAN—The depth will be fourteen feet.

MAJOR GENERAL GASCOIGNE—I was going to ask for fourteen feet. If you make it fourteen feet deep, I can only say that it will be of the utmost value, from a strategic point of view, to the country. I know the Imperial authorities look at it in that light also.

The CHAIRMAN—Have you ever been over that route?

MAJOR GENERAL GASCOIGNE—No.

The CHAIRMAN—But you know the general lie of the country?

MAJOR GENERAL GASCOIGNE—It is, of course, a thing we have looked at very closely both at home and here, from a strategic point of view. Parts of the country I have been over myself, but it is quite sufficient to look at the map to judge of the enormous value of this route, from a military point of view.

The CHAIRMAN—What depth of water would it require for the purpose of transporting your armaments through?

MAJOR GENERAL GASCOIGNE—Fourteen feet is what I should ask for. Fourteen feet would do me. I could do with less, but I should be very sorry to have less. Of course a Torpedo boat does not require the same depth of water, but, at the same time, to get the full value of the work, from a strategic point of view, fourteen feet is the least I should ask for.

The CHAIRMAN—What is the length of your vessels?

MAJOR GENERAL GASCOIGNE—I cannot tell you the full length, but the locks would have to be of considerable length. I am speaking from memory, but I think they should be not less than 120 feet.

The CHAIRMAN—Three hundred feet is the length proposed, and they are to be forty-five feet wide.

MAJOR GENERAL GASCOIGNE—That is excellent; nothing could be better. I feel perfectly sure that you would never regret the construction of such a canal. It would be of vast importance

The CHAIRMAN—You recollect that this Rideau Canal was built a great many years ago, with that object in view, by the Imperial authorities.

MAJOR GENERAL GASCOIGNE—Yes.

The CHAIRMAN—And if it was necessary then, do you consider it is equally necessary now?

MAJOR GENERAL GASCOIGNE—Much more necessary now, from many points of view which I think it would not be prudent for me to state here publicly, if you will just take what I have said from a strategic point of view. I cannot speak too highly of the value of this projected canal. I think it would be wise for me not to go into details, because I do not know how far my statements might be repeated abroad.

Hon. Mr. POWER—You may take it for granted that they would be stated as widely as possible.

Hon. Sir MACKENZIE BOWELL—And exaggerated.

MAJOR GENERAL GASCOIGNE—I should like to confine my statements to the vast importance of the project, as I look at it.

Mr. STEWART—Sir John Michel, who commanded Her Majesty's forces here in 1866, and Admiral Hope, Commander of the Squadron, went over this route the whole way by canoes and other ways, and when they came back they reported at a meeting held in Montreal that this canal was not only a commercial but a great military necessity for Canada. Are you of the same opinion?

MAJOR GENERAL GASCOIGNE—I am.

The CHAIRMAN—Do you know the opinion of the military authorities in England?

MAJOR GENERAL GASCOIGNE—I do. It would be looked upon with the utmost pleasure at home if this scheme were carried out.

Hon. Mr. POWER—I take it that it is chiefly from the Naval point of view. Since that time of which Mr. Stewart speaks, 1866, two railways have been built connecting the Ottawa with Lake Huron and of course for the purpose of transporting troops, for instance, the canal would not be nearly as useful or valuable. It is valuable now chiefly as a means of getting ships through.

The CHAIRMAN—And munitions of war.

Hon. Mr. POWER—They could be carried through by train. You would not think that it is very necessary to have this canal for the purpose of moving troops east or west?

MAJOR GENERAL GASCOIGNE—Of course it would be a most admirable thing even from that point of view.

Hon. Mr. POWER—But considering the fact that there are two railways running from Ottawa to Lake Huron, do you think the canal would be largely used for transporting troops in case there was any difficulty and it became necessary to move troops?

MAJOR GENERAL GASCOIGNE—It was not the movement of troops that I had in my mind chiefly.

The CHAIRMAN—But it would serve a purpose in that respect?

MAJOR GENERAL GASCOIGNE—Most unquestionably it would serve the purpose, but there are greater purposes than that which I have in mind.

The CHAIRMAN—I suppose you could not have a route more remote from the frontier for transportation than this Ottawa route?

MAJOR GENERAL GASCOIGNE—Certainly not, and it is just for that purpose that I consider it important.

Mr. MARCUS SMITH, M. Inst., C.E., called and examined.

The CHAIRMAN—Mr. Smith, you might tell us in a narrative form what you know about this canal.

Mr. SMITH—I am acquainted with this from the very commencement of the surveys in 1858 and 1860. Mr. Walter Shanly, the Engineer, commenced the surveys of this work in 1858, and they were completed by Mr. T. C. Clarke in 1860. I know both these gentlemen very well, and I know many of the assistants, as they have been working with me on other work; and I have seen most of the plans, soundings, profiles and so on deposited in the government office, and they are very complete. They are quite enough to make an estimate both as to the practicability of the work and the cost of construction.

That is the principal thing that I had to do with, just to ascertain that. I had tracings made, and went over the whole work. I found the first difficulty at Lake Nipissing. Lake Nipissing is about eighteen or twenty feet below the summit level of Trout Lake and the other Lakes on the Mattawa River. It was proposed by Mr. Clarke, who completed the surveys, to raise Lake Nipissing some ten or twelve feet and lower the other Lakes to meet it. I found that that cannot be done now. The Canadian Pacific Railway has been constructed alongside of Lake Nipissing at quite a low level, and the town of North Bay has been built: so that to raise the Lake now would flood a great many miles of that railway. Therefore that difficulty had to be provided for. The small rivers coming into the Mattawa River—the small feeders, are quite inadequate to supply a sufficient quantity of water for working this canal. Therefore there was no other way of getting it through, except finding how high Lake Nipissing could be raised without interfering with railway property and other property. I examined it some time ago; I found that the Lake could not be raised very much; in fact I propose now, from the calculations I have made, to keep the Lake up to the winter level. The Lake varies in level. In the fall of the year it is very low. The highest water is six or seven feet more than the lower level. I propose to keep the high level by damming the outlet of the Lake, and this can be done without interfering with any property, as nature has provided for it; I would not go beyond what nature does in raising the level of the Lake.

Hon. Sir MACKENZIE BOWELL—How would that affect the freshets in the Spring?

Mr. MARCUS SMITH—We have sluices, but there are more means than one to be taken with reference to the Spring freshets. Amongst the plans I found a profile of the canal from Lake Nipissing through to Trout Lake, a distance of about five miles, down to the Mattawa. From that profile I laid down the high water level of Lake Nipissing and I estimated the quantities from that, made a calculation right through so as to find the cost and added a considerable amount to the cost—added a million or a million and a half dollars to the cost of the work. This will make Lake Nipissing the summit level of the waterway, extending now over some fifty miles of water at the same level, all supplied from Lake Nipissing which is a Lake of some sixty miles in length and of very considerable depth in some places, so that we can regulate the level of the Lake by an outlet at both ends, both southward and eastward into the Mattawa River which goes into the Ottawa River. There is a great fall from the head waters of the Mattawa before it reaches the Ottawa, and I have lowered the line about eighteen feet and I can do it at Trout Lake; it is so deep that by lowering that, there is still plenty of water for navigation. In fact, Trout Lake is very deep, as Mr. Shanly gives soundings of 200 feet in some places without finding bottom.

Hon. Mr. SCOTT—What would be the depth of the cut between Nipissing and Trout Lake?

Mr. MARCUS SMITH—It varies very much. I think the highest cut is about thirty-two feet between Lake Nipissing and Trout Lake.

Hon. Mr. SCOTT—No physical difficulty?

Mr. MARCUS SMITH—Nothing except the cost of excavating and I have estimated all that by means of the surveys which have been made. They are so complete that I have been able to make a very reliable estimate from them.

Hon. Mr. SCOTT—Would there be a fall from Nipissing to Trout Lake, or would that be made level?

Mr. MARCUS SMITH—Trout Lake is lowered to the level of Lake Nipissing and the summit level will extend a considerable distance eastward of Trout Lake. Turtle Lake, which is the next lake to Trout Lake, is only two feet different in the level. I would lower the level of Trout Lake and the Lake adjoining it, Turtle Lake, so that they would be of the same level as Lake Nipissing. Then the summit level, when altered, would be 648 feet above the level of the sea, and when you get to the mouth of the Mattawa on the Ottawa River it has got down to 501—there is about 150 feet fall; consequently we have locks after we pass Trout Lake; we have to lock downwards towards the Ottawa River.

Now in making the calculations of work to be done and the estimate, I may say that Mr. Clark's quantities were got out for a depth of twelve feet of canal, and the depth on the lock sill of ten feet, and a width of not less than 100 feet at the bottom of the canal. My calculations have been made out for those dimensions, but lately it is proposed, instead of ten feet on the sill of the lock, to have fourteen feet, and that will necessitate the depth of the canal being at least fifteen feet or sixteen feet. Using the other calculations as a basis, I have been able to estimate the extra cost of that so far as it affects the same works, but it will incur other works, probably the depth of rivers will have to be dredged in some places—that I cannot tell without some further surveys.

Hon. Mr. Scott.—Will the increase in depth to fourteen feet leave a sufficiency of water between Trout Lake, Nipissing and Turtle Lakes?

Mr. Marcus Smith.—Yes.

Hon. Mr. Scott.—Between the old system of locks as originally contemplated and this new kind that is being proposed there is a saving in water.

Mr. Marcus Smith—It is only applicable where there is scarcity of water and where there is a very rapid fall; we have no necessity to do that at all. The inclination of the river is so gradual, it is only some ten or fifteen or twenty miles that we have to put a lock—one lock generally suffices at the same place. We propose to reduce the number of locks, as proposed by Mr. Clarke, and have them deeper. The average depth of the locks now on this survey is about eleven feet. We propose to make them as high as twenty feet, where it will be a saving. Where the nature of the fall is such that we want more than ten or twelve feet we will make all in one lock instead of two; we will be able to reduce the number of locks in that way. But there is no part of the line where there is any necessity for using what is called the pneumatic principle, lifting by compressed air. That can be done where there is scarcity of water and where there is a very rapid fall; for instance, at the locks at Ottawa here this might have been carried out all on the same level as it is at Sappers' Bridge, and would have been one drop to the river; but it was found rather an expensive process, this pneumatic work. There is a lot of machinery required. You have to have machinery for compressing the air, and machinery for working it. The way we are doing now is the simplest, always to use the water directly, simply by damming it and letting it fall into a basin; and there is no necessity in this case to use any other process. It is the cheapest process you could use; the only thing is you might gain time by reducing the number of locks and making them deeper, and time is a very great object in the cost of transportation. Now, with regard to the estimated cost of the work, I had to make it in two separate parts; there is the first from Ottawa to the Georgian Bay, which is entirely new work, and we have the measurements for that: the other part is from Ottawa to Montreal, which is Government canals. The Lachine canal, of course, requires no alteration. The intermediate canals between Lachine and Ottawa would have to be enlarged. There is only a depth of nine feet of water at present, and the length of lock 200 feet, and that I cannot make an estimate of without some survey.

Hon. Sir Mackenzie Bowell—What is the depth of the water in the Ottawa? Is it fourteen feet all the way?

Mr. Marcus Smith—I think there is only one place in the Ottawa, in going through these calculations, that we need to make any dredging at all for twelve feet, but there may be some more for fourteen feet, and that is the reason I cannot give a very close estimate of a fourteen foot canal. I can give an approximate estimate.

Hon. Sir Mackenzie Bowell—Is it rock?

Mr. Marcus Smith—I want a survey to find out. What is wanted now is a small sum of twenty or twenty-five thousand dollars to make a survey to find out whether there would be any extra work to do on account of altering the canal to fourteen feet. The canal would have to be fifteen and a half feet deep. They have plans in the government, plans that show the soundings of the rivers all through, but we want to find what the bottom is, whether it is earth or rock, to make an estimate of the cost of removing it. Of course if it is rock it will be very expensive work dredging and blasting. The cost I have estimated of the canal as originally proposed for a twelve foot depth of water in the canal and for 100 feet wide in the bottom and a length of lock 250 feet, ten feet on the sills, the whole from Ottawa to Georgian Bay, I have estimated that this could be done for about $15,000,000, and I made a very liberal estimate.

Hon. Sir Mackenzie Bowell—Is there no means devised to obviate the necessity of making the canal a foot deeper than the sill?

Mr. MARCUS SMITH—That is a question of navigation. The skippers would tell you they want one or two feet below the bottom of their keel.

Hon. Sir MACKENZIE BOWELL—I am speaking of the lock. You say that in order to have fourteen feet at the top of the mitre sill you must have the canal itself a foot deeper.

Mr. MARCUS SMITH—Not inside of the lock—outside the locks.

Hon. Sir MACKENZIE BOWELL—Yes. Has no invention or means been devised by which that could be avoided by making the sill on a level with the bottom of the canal by deepening where the swing would take place?

Mr. MARCUS SMITH—We could make the canal and the lock the same depth, but these skippers want two feet of water under their keel.

Hon. Sir MACKENZIE BOWELL—But if the sill was on a level with the bottom of the canal, then they would have the same quantity of water in passing into the lock as they would have in navigating the canal?

Mr. MARCUS SMITH—They would not require so much in the lock, that is all; their making the lock ten feet deep and the canal twelve feet deep is a saving; the canal is made two feet deeper.

As I was saying, the cost of that for ten feet on the sill and twelve feet canal from Ottawa to Georgian Bay I have estimated at $15,000,000, and I have checked that by Mr. Clarke's quantities; and I cannot alter the quantities, but where there was a curvature I have allowed more, because ships cannot go round a corner the same as a railway, as they are likely to go at a tangent—I have made a liberal estimate for that. The cost of enlarging the locks between Ottawa and Lachine I cannot say, because I have no data at all; but I have put down a million or a million and a half of dollars for altering the locks. They would have to be lengthened and deepened at Grenville and Carillon, and there are several locks.

Hon. Sir MACKENZIE BOWELL—What is the approximate cost over the fifteen millions of making it two feet deeper?

Mr. SMITH—I am coming to that in a moment. The difference between Mr. Shanly's estimate and Mr. Clarke's estimate is accounted for by the fact that Mr. Clarke's estimate was simply for the waterway; but there are harbours, piers, wharves, lighting, and all these things to be done just now. I have added all those in. I have put down a Million dollars for elevators, and I have put in a good sum for other things. There are lockkeeper's houses, and electricity, working the locks by electricity, and lighting the whole canal by electricity, and all those things together could be done for under Twenty Million dollars for the ten feet. I have gone over, as far as I had the data for making the calculation of the difference between the ten feet and the fourteen feet, and the difference varied considerably, according to the cuttings, from fifteen to forty per cent difference; but on the whole I think I would be very safe in saying that Five millions more would do the work; the work could be done for that much more. Of course the extra cost would only be in the canal and the locks themselves. There is all the lighting and elevators, and there would be no difference between the fourteen and ten feet in that respect. You would want more surveys to examine the rivers to find what the bottom is and what dredging would be required. I have no doubt there would be more dredging required for a fourteen foot canal than for a twelve foot canal, and some of that may be rock. It is sure to be rock in all the upper waters above the Ottawa. But there are only two parts on the Ottawa that require dredging for the twelve feet. Now, with regard to the depth, I do not know whether you want anything more on the Engineering question. That is my principal work; the question of practicability and cost is what I have been mainly working at. Of course there are other places besides cutting down the divide between Lake Nipissing and the Ottawa. At Mattawa they will have to change the locks there. They will have to be lowered partly. I have made the lock above it instead of below it and at Ottawa there will be considerable expense here in addition to what there would have been forty years ago. There are railways built and roads and everything and we will have a great many more bridges to make and that can only be ascertained by some extra surveys. Besides the actual engineering question, I have been in correspondence with people who are making works in other parts of the country and there is a great discussion now going on between what is called the deeper waterways—that is ships coming from the seas right up—that is a canal twenty-seven feet and and a canal fourteen feet deep. This is not properly a ship canal. It will have to be worked by barges and steam tugs, and the opinion now is getting very much in favour of working that way. It is contended by many forwarders and shipbuilders that work can be done cheaper that way than by the very large vessels that have been built on the Lakes this year. The reason is that it takes a great deal of water for the large vessels to run in. They want a great deal of water to run in in order to make it in a shorter time. But when they come to be intercepted in their passage by locks and all that, they waste time, and their expenses are going on all the time, and it is found that navigation by the lesser craft, the barges, is much cheaper.

Hon. Sir MACKENZIE BOWELL—Including transhipment?

Mr. MARCUS SMITH—I have made an allowance for transhipment at the foot of the French River at Georgian Bay. But I think now all the way from Lake Superior we could do without transhipment at all.

Hon. Mr. SCOTT—I think now they have found that the steam barge towed by a tug is a success.

Mr. MARCUS SMITH—Yes.

Hon. Mr. SCOTT—There is nothing so cheap as that mode, because there is no coal to burn and no hands to pay. It is like a moving store-house.

Mr. MARCUS SMITH—I have been in correspondence with a Company who are making surveys for building a canal from Lake Erie by the Ohio River, called the Lake Erie and Ohio Ship Canal, and I have here some information about it. I will read a portion of it with reference to the whaleback vessels and the canal :—

From a correspondence with Mr. Alexander McDougall, the inventor of the whaleback steamer and manager of the American Steel Barge Company, we quote the following statements relating to this subject :—

" There are thirty-five whalebacks in the lake country now which were built by this company. About one-half of them are 262 feet long, thirty-six feet beam and twenty-two feet depth of hold; their turrets, one at each end, are elevated above this twenty-two feet, sixteen feet. The other half of the boats are from 300 to 340 feet long. The first class are intended to be of the size to accommodate the new Canadian canals which are now being built at a cost of about $60,000,000.

" We think our type of vessel draws less water (consorts, when loaded, drawing three and a half feet, and can load to eighteen feet) and cost of transportation by them is cheaper than any other class of vessel already in use. A steamer towing two consorts makes the round trip from Duluth to Ashtabula in about twelve days with a cargo of about 6,500 tons in the three. My idea of your canal system from the lakes to Pittsburg, is that it would not be necessary to have them larger than the Canadian canals, which are of uniform size—270 feet long, forty-five feet wide and fourteen feet depth. In the future, a great many vessels will be adapted for this trade, and the difference in cost on their fourteen feet draught and that of their eighteen feet draught aimed at by our deep lake channels will be very slight, when steamers and barges are fitted specially for this purpose. I think a steamer and two consorts that will fill locks of the size you have adopted, can be made to carry very nearly as cheaply as anything that will ever be built for short runs like the lake, river and canal systems; this, besides, being of the general size adopted by the Canadian system, and some vessels will do in either trade.

" The steam whaleback that we have built—320 feet long, forty-two feet beam, carrying about 2,200 gross tons on fourteen feet, consorts of the same class without power except for pumping, steam windlasses, etc.—would carry about 2,500 gross tons of fourteen feet. The same beam and depth might apply to vessels up to 340 feet long. The same depth of hold and turrets and that portion above water would be about the same in vessels of the 340-foot class, as in those of the 262-foot class. Then without cargo, the consorts, to the top of their houses, would be about thirty-five feet above water, while the steamers would be, to the top of the smoke-stack, about fifty-five feet above water, and the masts, to carry lights on the steamers, would necessarily have to be sixty feet above water."

It will thus be seen that for all classes of whaleback steamers they can pass under the height for fixed bridges, namely, forty-five feet, by hinging their smoke-stacks and arranging their topmasts for lowering to that elevation.

Cost of construction and operation of vessels of the Whaleback type.

Upon this subject Mr. McDougall says: "In regard to the cost and operating expenses of steamers and consorts 262 feet long, thirty-six feet beam and twenty-two feet depth of hold, such vessels would carry, on fourteen feet, a steamer 2,000 net tons (of 2,000 pounds) and the consorts or barges about 2,300 net tons each on fourteen feet draught, and would cost about $42 per ton of their carrying capacity, with sufficient power in the steamer to tow two consorts loaded eight miles an hour. It would cost to operate them in the lake trade about $42,000 per year, including all the operating expenses, insurance, repairs and management, but not the cost of handling the cargo. The custom in the lake country is, ore cargoes the ship pays for trimming two and a half cents; unloading fifteen cents. Most all other cargoes except coal are paid for at these prices. Coal is always free to the vessel at both ends. Iron ore is classed as gross tons, 2,240 pounds, while nearly all other freights are based upon 2,000 pounds. The figures and cost given you here would apply to smaller boats nearly in proportion either for a twelve foot draught or less if the boats were designed for that special size.

"Taking as a basis our smaller classes of whalebacks 264 feet long it would cost about the same to operate steamers or consorts up to 340 feet; and I think it would cost no more to carry cargoes by lake and canal with a much smaller vessel than 264 feet long, if specially made of a standard size, and adapted for the canal and lake trade. We are to-day building in our yard four large ships of the whaleback type, of the following dimensions : one 404 feet, two 380 feet and one 360 feet long; but I do not expect to get any better results from them than the last steamer we turned out, which has to her credit the best record ever known, and she is only 320 feet long. Where vessels are delayed or slowed on account of canal or other causes, their first high cost interferes with their cheap operating and net profits; and I am of opinion that a smaller vessel than the regular lake carrier can be used for lake and canal trade more profitably than the large steamer of modern construction for lake trade.

"The great newspaper criticism of the large lake steamship and its advantages over the smaller vessel has been overdrawn. I think they have reached the highest point in size and possibly too large on some of them for such a short run (less than 1,000 miles), and I am of the opinion that steamers and barges first mentioned here, or even smaller, will show better net results on low rates of transportation than the very expensive large steamers with their high valuation, recently built for the lake trade; and that a vessel adapted for even a twelve feet draught can be made a very profitable vessel for the lake trade, and particularly so should they become a standard size and built on modern ideas, and when fitted and intended for canal and lake trade."

That meets exactly the conditions of our canal, and the coasting trade is very largely done in barges.

Hon. Mr. POWER—What draught are those smaller sized vessels he speaks of there?

Mr. MARCUS SMITH—They are ten feet draught, and the other which he calls the canal system is the fourteen feet draught, and I think it would be better for the sake of the difference of five million dollars or more to make this canal fourteen feet, and we would have all the canals of the Dominion of the same type; and the same sort of vessels would do for either.

Hon. Mr. BOULTON—You think there is water enough for a fourteen foot canal?

Mr. MARCUS SMITH—Oh, yes, plenty of water.

Hon. Mr. Power—Your vessel would come from Chicago, Duluth, Port Arthur, or Fort William and could go down to Montreal without breaking bulk.

Mr. Marcus Smith—Oh, yes. I do not know at what points they can commence with tugs and barges. They certainly can do so at Sault Ste. Marie, because by Sault Ste Marie and Georgian Bay they are partially sheltered all the way, but on Lake Superior I am not so sure what they could do.

Hon. Mr. Power—They go down from Duluth by the Sault Ste. Marie Canal. The only point I wanted to get at was that there would be no transhipment involved between Port Arthur or Duluth or Chicago and Montreal or Quebec.

Mr. Marcus Smith—I think not. You can go right through with the fourteen foot vessels, and the whale-back type is made to stand that, and I think by loading at Duluth or Port Arthur and coming through to Montreal or Quebec that it will be done at probably at one-third the cost that any railway system could do it. They can tranship goods at one-third per cent of what the railway companies charge.

Hon. Mr. Boulton—What do you estimate the fourteen foot canal can be built for?

Mr. Marcus Smith—Twenty-five million dollars. For the ten foot I am sure of twenty million, but there are some surveys to be made in order to make a close estimate.

Hon. Sir Mackenzie Bowell—That includes elevators, wharfs and terminal facilities?

Mr. Marcus Smith—Yes, everything connected with it.

Hon. Mr. Boulton—And what amount of power would be generated for the enterprise?

Mr. Marcus Smith—In the aggregate you have as much power, and it is better distributed; but besides the power I have estimated from opening and operating the canal, a great deal of that could be disposed of to advantage. But I have estimated for twenty horse power in opening and shutting canals, and I have taken a fall of twenty feet. That includes the lighting and everything.

The Chairman—Have you made calculations of the amount of electrical power that can be had from that work?

Mr. Marcus Smith—It is estimated they can have more than they have from Niagara. We have plenty of power.

The Chairman—Could not electrical power be employed as a motive power for these vessels?

Mr. Marcus Smith—Yes. You could not have it with the trolley system, of course; you would have to carry the motive power. No doubt it could be done, and no doubt it will be done, and the water power will generate electricity.

Hon. Sir Mackenzie Bowell—In some of the earlier reports, if I remember correctly—it was Shanly's, I think—it was stated they could not obtain water sufficient.

Mr. Marcus Smith—That is, without cutting down the divide.

Hon. Sir Mackenzie Bowell—Oh, yes; that difficulty has been overcome now.

Mr. Marcus Smith—Yes. That would cost one million and a half. Then speaking of the original system of raising the lake fourteen or fifteen feet I doubt if it is practicable, and if it were practicable I doubt if they could maintain it. I think probably the evaporation would be more than the supply for the lake.

Hon. Mr. De Boucherville—But as it is there is a portion of the water goes through French River?

Mr. Marcus Smith—Yes.

Hon. Mr. De Boucherville—When you start the canal you will have a dam at the head of French River.

Mr. Marcus Smith—Besides what we use for the canal, for the boats and navigation, the fall, the outlet, there is a volume of water going all the time out of French River. We want water below as well as above.

Hon. Mr. De Boucherville—But as it is now a large quantity of water goes through French River.

Mr. Marcus Smith—Oh, yes.

Hon. Mr. Scott—That is the outlet of Lake Nipissing.

Mr. Marcus Smith—Nipissing is about sixty-five feet higher than the Georgian Bay and we would have three or four locks on French River.

Hon. Mr. De Boucherville—You would regulate the flow of the water in French River.

Mr. Marcus Smith—Yes, we would maintain the Lake on a certain level, but when there is a flood there is an overflow.

Hon. Sir Mackenzie Bowell—What is the distance from Lake Nipissing to the Georgian Bay via French River?

Mr. Marcus Smith—It is about fifty miles.

Hon. Mr. De Boucherville—How many dams would you require on French River?

Mr. Marcus Smith—The French River is remarkably favourable for navigation. I have been up and down it frequently, and I could not observe any current in it at all. It is a series of Lakes with falls between them.

Hon. Mr. De Boucherville—It is very picturesque, I believe.

Mr. Marcus Smith—It is, but there is nothing but rock all the way. You ask the number of locks on the French River. There are four, and the rise is about sixty-five feet.

The Chairman—What is the estimated cost of constructing a canal fourteen feet in depth?

Mr. Marcus Smith—For fourteen feet of navigation there may be contingencies that could only be ascertained by means of a survey, but I roughly approximate the cost when I say $25,000,000. It would not take much to examine the nature of the material to be dredged, &c.

Hon. Mr. Power—What is the depth of the canals between Ottawa and the St. Lawrence River now?

Mr. Marcus Smith—Nine feet and the locks are only 200 feet long.

Hon. Mr. Power—Should we not recommend in the first instance the deepening of these canals?

Hon. Mr. De Boucherville—That would not be needed unless we had the rest of the canal.

Hon. Mr. Power—It would be useful for shipments from Ottawa. This City is becoming a great railway centre, and the enlargement of the canal would help shipments from here to the coast.

The Chairman—The canals will have to be enlarged and the river in some places deepened.

Hon. Sir Mackenzie Bowell—With a fourteen foot canal could you not load a vessel here and ship direct to Liverpool?

Mr. Marcus Smith—I do not know that sea-going vessels would be able to come up to Ottawa.

Hon. Mr. Prowse—There are plenty of them that draw less than fourteen feet.

Mr. Marcus Smith—With regard to the question of enlarging the canals between here and Montreal, I did not make an estimate, besides I do not know under what circumstances they are to be enlarged.

The Committee adjourned.

THE SENATE,
OTTAWA 12th May, 1898.

The COMMITTEE met this day.

The Hon. Mr. Clemow. Chairman.

Mr. JAMES MELDRUM.—I am a Member of the Institution of Civil Engineers of Great Britain, and Head of the Foreign Department of S. Pearson & Son, Limited, who, I think, are the largest Contractors of public works in the world.

We have been approached by Mr. McLeod Stewart as to whether we will undertake the construction of the Georgian Bay Canal, and my answer has been that provided the financial position is satisfactorily settled we are willing to undertake the construction of the works on a basis to be arranged with the Company, and to give these works the skill and attention which have proved satisfactory to other Governments. To establish our position as to our ability to carry out these works, I propose to give you briefly a list of some important works which we have recently constructed or are now constructing. We have recently completed the Blackwall Tunnel for the London County Council at a cost of about one million sterling, for which service the President of our Company has been created a Baronet. We have just completed the drainage of the valley of the city of Mexico by canal 25 miles long, and in places 90 feet deep, which has changed the whole area from a swamp into dry land, at a cost of about $10,000,000. At present we are constructing for the Admiralty of Great Britain, Dover Harbour at a cost of about three millions sterling, which will convey to you that we are on the Admiralty list, which is the highest honour that a Contractor can get. We are constructing Vera Cruz Harbour for the Mexican Government. We have railway and dock contracts in England amounting, exclusive of the Dover Harbour contract, to three or four millions sterling. We have just completed an arrangement with the Mexican Government by which we take over from them the Tehuantepec Railway from the Pacific to the Atlantic. We propose to build large harbours at each end and divert the whole trade of the Pacific to the Atlantic to a new route. More within your own knowledge, we built and are part owners of the Halifax Graving Dock.

The CHAIRMAN.—What did that cost?

Mr. MELDRUM.—I could not at this moment say.

Hon. Mr. POWER.—It is a good work.

Mr. MELDRUM.—I believe it is the only satisfactory Graving Dock on the East coast of America. Besides what I have mentioned we are at present in negotiation with the Egyptian, Chilian, Argentine and Uruguayan Governments for other large works, amounting in all to about fifteen millions sterling. We have works in hand to over ten millions sterling, and are negotiating for fifteen millions more. As to the scheme before us, I can only say that I have read over the various descriptions of the works which have been prepared by the distinguished Engineers engaged on the survey, and from these I see no engineering difficulty to prevent their execution. As to the Commercial aspect, I think it would be presumptuous of me to offer any ideas at all to your Committee. You are in a far better position than I to form any idea as to the commercial aspect. Our idea is this: that if the Canadian Government, the Provinces and, probably, also the Home Government gave a certain guarantee on the proposed capital that we could undertake to assist in raising the capital in London, and in forming a Company there, and ourselves execute the whole work. It seems to me undoubted that you are the best people to appreciate the advantage of such a canal: and that therefore, if you are prepared to back your opinion in cash in the nature of a subsidy or guarantee, we are prepared to execute the works. I have attempted to give you an outline to show you that we have back-bone enough to carry through such a scheme. As to the advantages of canals, some years ago I had occasion to report to one of the London

Banks on a railway in Holland and there I found, what is generally known, that for low grade traffic which does not require any great speed, railways have no possible chance with a canal.   Only a few of the through lines in Holland pay, where they compete against canals.   I think I said I had not been over this route, I had been delayed in arriving here, and therefore am not in a position to criticise or give any opinion on the route or on the engineering details.   Mr. McLeod Stewart has asked me whether for such a scheme if the Government propose to guarantee the interest on the capital, it would be possible to arrange that interest should commence not on the beginning of the works, but on the opening of canal.   On that point I have only to say that it is often done in Great Britain : it could be arranged that the interest on the bonds could be paid by the contractors during construction and, of course, added to the cost of the contract, so that the guarantee of the Government would only become effective when the canal was open.

The CHAIRMAN.—Have you any idea of what length of time it would take to build the canal?

Mr. MELDRUM.—I have not formed any opinion at present.   I might mention that we are offered by the British Government ten years to do the Dover Works. We propose to do them in seven.   But at Dover we have only three points at which we can attack the works.   In the case of this canal, we could attack them at probably over 100 points, so that I think three or four years would be ample for the construction.

The CHAIRMAN.—Have you made any calculation of what the proposed cost would be?

Mr. MELDRUM.—I am not in a position to criticise the report of the Engineers who have been before you.   I notice that one Engineer estimates the works at $25,000,000, another at $17,000,000.   I am now getting from Mr. McLeod Stewart certain data as to the cost of works in this country, from which I hope at an early day to be able to calculate which of these estimates is the correct one.

Hon. Mr. POWER.—I do not think, Mr. Chairman, that the two estimates were made at the same time or based on exactly the same condition of things.

The CHAIRMAN.—No, I think not.   (To Mr. Meldrum)—Have you seen Mr. Clarke's?

Mr. MELDRUM.—I met Mr. Clarke in New York, and discussed the whole scheme with him.   This morning I met Mr. Marcus Smith and discussed some of his figures.

Hon. Sir MACKENZIE BOWELL.—It was Mr. Marcus Smith who gave the estimate of $25,000,000—that was the full completion, and with other completions too.

Mr. MELDRUM.—That I believe includes the completion of the canal down to Montreal.

The CHAIRMAN.—Yes.

Hon. Sir MACKENZIE BOWELL.—How long a period do you ask the Government to guarantee the interest?

Mr. MELDRUM.—My own belief, from the documents put before me, is that if you gave a guarantee you would never be called on to pay it; if Mr. McLeod Stewart's figures are in any way reliable there would be no necessity for a guarantee at all. It is only a safeguard for raising the capital.

Hon. Sir MACKENZIE BOWELL.—But still you would want a guarantee in order to assist you in raising the capital, and for how long a period would that be?

Mr. MELDRUM.—For as long as the canal required it.

Hon. Sir MACKENZIE BOWELL.—As long as the issue of the bonds, you mean?

Mr. MELDRUM.—I mean so long as the canal was not paying a sufficient net revenue.

Hon. Sir MACKENZIE BOWELL.—That would mean a perpetual guarantee.

Mr. MELDRUM.—A perpetual guarantee : it would not be effective I hope, after the first year.

Hon. Sir MACKENZIE BOWELL.—The reason I ask that question is that Governments have guaranteed the interest upon bonds for a certain number of years.

Mr. MELDRUM.—That is so ; we have the same condition elsewhere.

Hon. Mr. Power.—Suppose the Government guaranteed the interest for say 25 years, would that be satisfactory?

Mr. Meldrum.—Quite.

The Chairman.—Or even, 20 years.

Mr. Meldrum.—20 would be quite satisfactory.

The Chairman.—That is the limit we named before : and I understood it was only to be paid six years after the canal was commenced.

Mr. Meldrum.—That could be arranged.

Hon. Sir Mackenzie Bowell.—I see very little difference in that, because according to this gentleman's statement the contractors would pay the interest on the bonds or the interest on the money loaned, until the canal is completed, after which the interest they have paid is added to the cost of the canal.

Hon. Mr. Power.—But Mr. Meldrum's statement is a guarantee that the work will be completed promptly ; that is the important feature about it.

The Chairman.—I understood this guarantee was to commence six years after the completion of the canal.

Mr. Meldrum.—No ; commence on the completion of the canal.

Hon. Sir Mackenzie Bowell.—That is very reasonable.

The Chairman.—Altogether you view the project as one which ought to engage the attention of the authorities ?

Mr. Meldrum.—Most decidly. My own opinion is that it wants to be strongly pressed on the Government here in order to get them to give their support in one form or other, and with that support the matter can be carried through immediately.

The Chairman.—I suppose we would be justified in reporting to the Senate that your proposition to your Company would be of the nature you have indicated here?

Mr. Meldrum.—Certainly. I think it is fully understood that the canal Company shall have the right to own and work their own barges during the life of the canal itself, for commercial purposes.

Hon. Sir Mackenzie Bowell.—If the Company had the right during the life of the canal to use their own barges that would be free of tolls ?

•   Mr. Meldrum.—No, like other people they would have to pay tolls. The canal company has to keep up its canal out of its own earnings, and whatever way you take it all comes to the same thing.

Hon. Sir Mackenzie Bowell.—The use of the canal for the purpose of constructing and repairing and doing things of that kind would be fair, but when they would have the use of the canal free of toll for commercial purposes, to do the whole commercial business of the canal between the waters of Lake Huron and Montreal, would they give the credit to their earnings—if they were to have the free use they certainly would not.

Mr. Meldrum.—They are bound under clause two of article 23 of the contract to charge themselves, because that is a clause against preferential rates, so that they would be bound to charge themselves the same rates as any others.

Hon. Sir Mackenzie Bowell.—But would you give the indebtedness of the Company credit for the amount you would earn, in order to reduce the liabilities of those who guarantee the bonds.

Mr. Meldrum.—You would be bound to debit the Company with the same rates that you charge to other people.

Hon. Sir Mackenzie Bowell.—Would that be considered as an earning of the canal, to go and be placed against interest or capital ?

Mr. Meldrum.—Undoubtedly so. As to that matter of preferential rates there is a clause there which prevents preferential rates. I have discussed the same point with the Mexican Government, and there is only one remark I would like to make on it. We put it to the Ministers in Mexico whether preferential rates would prevent your giving a special rate to a man who had a large amount of cargo. You could not expect a man having 100 tons to get the same rates as a man having 10,000 tons. You could give 10,000 tons a preferential rate. Would that be prohibited ? The Government answered no, it would not be prohibited ; but if any other person wants a rate for 10,000 tons you must carry that cargo for the same rate as you have carried the same cargo for other people. You must place every one on the same footing.

Hon. Sir MACKENZIE BOWELL.—That is the principle of the Customs Act.

Mr. MELDRUM.—You may give special rates, but you must apply to every one equally.

The CHAIRMAN.—Did you give any attention to the electrical advantages?

Mr. MELDRUM.—I have not received from Mr. McLeod Stewart a statement of the power that can be obtained or the power—that may be marketable.

———

ORMOND HIGMAN, Chief Dominion Electrician, appeared before the Committee and was examined as follows :—

Mr. STEWART.—You have been going over this route for the last 25 years. Will you explain before this Committee about the advantages from an electrical standpoint.

Mr. HIGMAN.—Well, I have only been over a portion of the route, the portion between Mattawa and Ottawa. I have gone pretty thoroughly over that portion of it. In a letter to yourself some two or three years ago I stated that I thought the water for electrical purposes on the Ottawa was equal to that of Niagara. I would like to amend that statement now by saying that I think it infinitely superior. While at Niagara the power is concentrated at the one point, and could only be used within a radius of thirty or forty miles, the Ottawa affords power all along the 400 miles at very convenient distances. We expect in the near future—I suppose I might venture the statement that within ten years electricity will be used entirely on our long distance railways; that is for passenger traffic. The Canadian Pacific runs parallel and close to the proposed canal the whole distance from Lake Nipissing to Montreal, and that part could undoubtedly be used for the purposes of railway traffic and it could also be used for propelling barges along the canal. At the Chats Rapids, where there is an unlimited amount of power. It seems to me electric power could be used for the smelting of iron. That I think has been proven now to be feasible, and the country all along the route is full of iron, and this electrical power could be used in place of fuel for the smelting of iron. I of course made no calculation as to the amount of horse power, the quantity of electrical power that could be gotten out of these different rapids, but it is enormous. We have some evidence of it close at the door here, two of the rapids are being used only partially, a very small fraction in fact of the power is being used at Ottawa and Deschenes, and that condition of things exists all along the route.

The CHAIRMAN.—There is no doubt about it, every few miles from Montreal it could be utilized.

Mr. HIGMAN.—Yes, it occurs at such convenient intervals that a generating station will stretch out twenty or thirty miles in each direction, and then it meets the power from the other stations, and so you get a continuous current right along the whole route, and it could be used as I say for railway purposes; no doubt about that, and the manufacture of calcium carbide for Acetylene gas, and a great many things. Of course there is an endless variety of uses to which it could be put.

The CHAIRMAN.—That only extends to the Mattawa. That is all you know about.

Mr. HIGMAN.—Yes, that is all. I know the country between Ottawa and Mattawa very thoroughly and there can be no doubt at all as to the magnificent water powers that exist along the route.

Hon. Sir MACKENZIE BOWELL.—How far is it from Mattawa to Lake Nipissing?

Mr. HIGMAN.—I do not know.

Mr. MARCUS SMITH.—I do not remember. I think it is about 40 or 50 miles.

Mr. HIGMAN.—There is no doubt that if a Company owning the franchise building this canal—if one were to present them with a water power equal to the Niagara they would think it was a very fine thing, but the Ottawa condition of things is far superior.

Hon. Sir MACKENZIE BOWELL—Mr. Smith, in his calculation and estimate of the cost of construction of the canal took into consideration the use of electricity along the whole route.

The CHAIRMAN.—I suppose that electricity could be employed during the construction to advantage.

Mr. HIGMAN.—Oh, yes.

Hon. Sir MACKENZIE BOWELL.—It could be used for excavation.

The CHAIRMAN.—It would save a good deal of manual labour.

HENRY K. WICKSTEED appeared before the committee and was examined as follows :—

Mr. STEWART.—You are a Civil Engineer by profession ?

Mr. WICKSTEED.—Yes.

Mr. STEWART.—And you have been over the whole of this route almost ?

Mr. WICKSTEED.—The greater part of it.

Mr. STEWART.—Will you explain to this Committee the advantages and practicability and feasibility of this scheme.

Mr. WICKSTEED.—I do not know that I can add much more to my written testimony and Mr. T. C. Clark's report. I can endorse all that was said in those reports.

The CHAIRMAN.—You have seen nothing since to change your opinion ?

Mr. WICKSTEED.—No, I think rather the other way. I have been impressed with the feasibility of it.

Hon. Sir MACKENZIE BOWELL.—Your opinion has already been given in that report.

Mr. WICKSTEED.—Yes, I have been quoted several times and I sent you a written answer to Mr. McLeod Stewart's question.

Mr. STEWART.—You answered those questions ?

Mr. WICKSTEED.—Yes.

The CHAIRMAN.—Did you treat on the electrical part of it ?

Mr. WICKSTEED.—Incidentally. I am not an expert in electrical work. I did not enlarge on that.

The CHAIRMAN.—What is your opinion as to the expediency and feasibility of making it a fourteen foot canal ?

Mr. WICKSTEED.—As to the feasibility I think there is no question whatever.

The CHAIRMAN.—When were you over the route last ?

Mr. WICKSTEED.—I was over the greater part of it last winter with Mr. Stewart.

The CHAIRMAN.—Is this report of yours predicated on that ?

Mr. WICHSTEED.—It is since that time.

The CHAIRMAN.—A report was made by Mr. Clark and Mr. Shanly a great many years ago. Had you anything to do with that ?

Mr. WICKSTEED.—No, I had nothing to do with that. I have seen Mr Clark since, and I have had his report, and I think I mastered it pretty thoroughly.

Hon. Mr. PROWSE.—Is there a possibility of making a twenty foot canal.

Mr. WICKSTEED.—A twenty foot canal was my first proposition. I am the father of that proposition. I always leaned towards the twenty foot canal. The testimony of Major Symons, who has been employed by the Deep Water Commission to inquire into the proper scheme of navigation for the New York state canals and that sort of thing, seemed to favour a lighter draught. He seemed to think a fourteen foot canal would be as economical as a twenty foot, on account of this new scheme of hauling barges behind a tug.

Hon. Mr. PROWSE.—Would it not necessitate transhipment? If you had a twenty foot canal the large ships could go right through without transhipment ?

4—3

Mr. WICKSTEED.—That was my first idea, but there was objections to that. They say that the crews at sea are not the proper crews to have in inland water.

The CHAIRMAN.—The cost of a ship is very much larger in proportion to the cost of steam barges.

Hon. Mr. PROWSE.—What difference would that make? You would not want the steam barges at all.

Mr. WICKSTEED.—In the case of the steam barges they are never at rest; when they get to their destination and unload they are immediately taken back.

Hon. Mr. PROWSE.—I understand it is giving a good deal of employment and traffic to the people along the route.

Mr. WICKSTEED.—Yes.

Hon. Mr. PROWSE.—There is no more expensive port to unload at than Montreal; all shipowners will tell you that.

Mr. WICKSTEED.—I think the canal would be carried down to Montreal by the Back River about four miles behind Montreal.

Hon. Sir MACKENZIE BOWELL.—Is that not called Black River?

Mr. WICKSTEED.—No, it is Back River.

Hon. Sir MACKENZIE BOWELL.—But you would have to canal that?

Mr. WICKSTEED.—Yes, there are only two rapids on it.

The CHAIRMAN.—Is there plenty of water except the two rapids.

Mr. WICKSTEED.—Yes, plenty of water excepting the two rapids. I think that is what it would come to, and that would make another harbour behind Montreal fully equal or rather larger than Montreal harbour itself.

The CHAIRMAN.—I suppose by incorporating what you said before we would have your statement?

Mr. WICKSTEED.—I do not think I can add anything to it. It was written only a few days ago.

The Committee adjourned.

LIST OF QUESTIONS.

LIST OF QUESTIONS SENT TO VARIOUS PERSONS TO ELICIT INFOR-
MATION RESPECTING THE PROPOSED WATERWAY BETWEEN THE
WATERS OF THE ST. LAWRENCE AND LAKE HURON.

1. Is it your opinion that the construction of this canal will benefit the Commerce of the Dominion generally ?

2. How would the construction of this canal affect the North-west and
Manitoba ?

3. What would be the trade which would be done through it and how would it
affect the Provinces of Ontario and Quebec ?

4. What would be the effect of the construction of this canal on the trade of the
Cities of Montreal and Quebec ?

5. To what extent would the opening of this water way be beneficial in developing local resources ?

6. What effect would the working of the canal have on the traffic of the
Canadian Pacific and Arnprior and Parry Sound Railways, and on the extension of
railway construction in Northern Ontario ?

7. How would its construction affect the lumber and pulp wood industries?

8. What effect would it have on development of mining and smelting industries
in the Ottawa Valley, and especially of iron mining ?

9. What effect would the opening of this waterway have on the cost of transportation of grain and produce from the Great Lakes to the Atlantic Seaboard and
New England States ?

10. How will cost of construction of the canals compare with cost in 1860 ?

11. What will be the length of the season of navigation ? and how will it compare with that at Sault Ste. Marie and Montreal ?

12. What advantages has the route considered as a means of military defence ?

13. Any information of importance as to the feasibility, financial prospects, or
results of the undertaking not included in the foregoing questions.

4—3½

ANSWERS TO THE FOREGOING QUESTIONS GIVEN BY THE FOLLOW-
ING PARTIES, AMONG OTHERS, AND THEIR REPLIES ARE HERETO
ATTACHED.

Sir Wm. Van Horne, K.C.M.G., President of the Canadian Pacific Railway
Company.
Walter Shanly, Esq., C.E.
Wm. White, Esq., Pembroke.
R. W. Shepherd, Esq., Managing Director Ottawa River Navigation Company.
L. P. Snyder, Esq., Manager Traders' Bank, North Bay.
Geo. G. Dustan, Esq., Dartmouth, N.S.
R. Adams Davey, C.E., and
H. K. Wicksteed, C.E., of Cobourg.

———

1. Yes.
2. Anything tending to lessen the cost of transportation between Manitoba and
the North-west, and the Seaboard, must unquestionably have a beneficial effect.
3. Its trade would chiefly be in grain, forest products, minerals and other
coarse freights. The water powers it would afford should result in the establish-
ment of important industries along its course in Ontario and Quebec.
4. It should greatly increase the trade of Montreal and Quebec and other Canadian seaports.
5. By the utilization of the water powers it would afford, and by the cheapness
of transportation.
6. So far as the Canadian Pacific is concerned it should create more traffic than
it would take away. I cannot speak concerning the other railway mentioned.
7. It should result in the utilization of all kinds of forest products, some of
which are not now available because of the cost of carriage.
8. It should have a most favourable effect on the development of the mineral
resources in the Ottawa Valley and beyond.
9. It should result in a a reduction of the cost of transportation to some extent;
I am unable to make an estimate.
10. It should be much less because of improved methods and appliances.
11. I should think about the same as at Sault Ste. Marie.
12. I am not a military man.

WM. VAN HORNE.

31st March, 1898.

———

1. I believe that it would do so.
2. The construction of the canal could not but affect the North-west beneficially
in cheapening transportation, especially in affording cheap transportation to the
waterpowers along the route. The Ottawa Valley might become the greatest flour-
milling country in the world.
3. The trade would, of course, chiefly be in cereals. The effect on both Provinces
would be beneficial, as stimulating trade generally.
4. Grain from Lakes Michigan and Superior could be laid down in Montreal at
a lower rate, and in Quebec at no higher rate, than the lowest rates ever reached
between the Lakes and New York.
5. It could not be otherwise than beneficial in developing local resources, but to
attempt to estimate to what extent would be mere guess-work.
6. Whatever benefits the country generally will not harm the railways. The
New York Central Railway alongside the free Erie Canal increases its traffic and its

earnings year by year, and will still do so when the canal has been improved (a work now in progress) to 9 feet draft.

7. Very beneficially, certainly.

8. The successful development of such industries is mainly dependent on cheap transportation. That, the projected navigation would supply.

9. No very marked effect unless a corresponding waterway was opened from Lake St. Louis direct to Lake Champlain.

10. The cost of the whole undertaking would not be less now than the highest official estimate on record.

11. As between the Lakes, generally, and Montreal, the "season" would be some ten days shorter by way of the Ottawa than by way of the Welland Canal.

12. A valuable auxiliary provided the "flag" also holds the naval supremacy of the Lakes.

13. 1st—*Feasibility.* Quite feasible for a 9-foot navigation.

2nd—*Financial Prospects.* Direct money returns, or profits, on outlay not to be looked for. It must be a free highway beyond such toll as may be necessary for the proper maintenance of the works.

3rd—*Results of the Undertaking.* These only to be considered as to their effect upon the commerce of the country. The answers here made to most of the queries incline to the belief that the effect and results of the projected line of navigation would be for the general advantage of Canada.

W. SHANLY.

26th March, 1898.

———

1. Most decidedly.

2. It would shorten the route between head of Lake Superior and Montreal materially, and give perfectly safe navigation from mouth of French River to Montreal.

3. It might not do much for Ontario, except the northern part of it. But it would, in my opinion, make another New York of Montreal.

4. Impossible to over-estimate the value of this canal to these cities.

5. I think it would develop the Ottawa Valley immensely, find a market for the hardwood and pulp-woods which are now practically useless owing to high freight rates.

6. Don't think it would materially affect these roads as I am satisfied the increased population that would result from the construction of the canal would furnish these roads with all the traffic they could handle.

8. Have already answered this, but may explain more fully that with increased facilities for shipping large quantities of maple, birch, ash and other hardwood that is not now cut at all (and of which there is an almost inexhaustible supply) would be cut and shipped.

8. Must benefit iron mining especially. I know of one of the best and largest iron deposits within 40 miles of this Town, and half a mile from Ottawa River, that is now perfectly useless, owing to high freight rates, that must become immensely valuable if canal is built.

9. It seems beyond a doubt that the cost would be greatly reduced.

10. Cannot say. Should think, with modern explosives, and the advance made in all works of this kind, the cost, now, should be much less.

11. Six or seven months—about the same as the Soo and Montreal.

WM. WHITE.

———

1. Yes, undoubtedly.

2. It would add immensely to the means of transporting grain and greatly lessen the cost of its carriage by shortening the distance from the West to Montreal and Quebec, and generally improve the transportation trade.

3. Grain, lumber, pulp-wood and manufactured goods would find a market more readily from the west. The North-eastern portion of Ontario and the Province of Quebec would derive great advantages.

4. It would tend to improve the trade of Montreal and Quebec. This waterway would be a great opponent to the Erie Canal system, and would, no doubt, attract a large portion of the grain trade which now goes by New York.

5. The construction of this water way would open up the country and be the means of establishing villages and towns *en route*. The numerous water powers along the line of route would be the means whereby unlimited electric power could be developed.

6. The construction of this waterway would develop and settle the North-eastern portion of Ontario, which would greatly benefit the railways already constructed.

7. Most advantageously, by giving great opportunity for erecting Mills at numerous points.

8. It would have a good effect in developing mining and smelting industries and affording cheap means of transport to low class freight of that kind.

10. The cost of construction, as compared with cost in 1860, should be much less, because the machinery and appliances for constructing such work now, are vastly improved, and the work ought to be effected not only at less cost, but also much more expeditiously.

11. The length of the season of navigation should average seven months—from the 25th April to 25th November.

12. The route would be of great advantage for military and defence, as a means of passing gun-boats quickly through the heart of Canada, from the Sea to the Great Lakes.

R. W. SHEPHERD,
Man. Dir. Ottawa River Navigation Co.

1. I certainly do. From what I have been able to learn, fully eighty per cent of the grain from the Western States reaches the seaboard by the Erie Canal, a much longer route than the one referred to above. Montreal is nearer Europe than New York, and still *via* the Ottawa Valley Montreal is 340 miles nearer Chicago than *via* the St. Lawrence route. I am of the opinion that a much larger share of the grain trade from the west would be secured by the opening up of the northern waterway, which is at once feasible, and, from a national standpoint, possessing many advantages over the St. Lawrence.

2. The North-west Provinces would be given a much shorter all-water route to Fort William than the one now used, and which would necessarily cheapen transportation for freight westward, besides giving them a shorter route to the sea for their products. Besides the advantage of a shorter haul from Fort William, much less time in proportion to the distance, is occupied in reaching Montreal, owing to the long stretches of inland waterways in almost their natural state, which would not be affected at all by the speed of steamers passing through them, whereas the same speed in coursing through some of the canals on the other and existing routes would cause havoc to the banks. It has been said that a steamer leaving Chicago by the northern route would reach Liverpool from Chicago in the time occupied in reaching New York by the Erie Canal.

3. The country through which the canal would pass is filled with mineral, lumber, hardwoods of various kinds, many of which are to-day being exported to the British Isles from Maine, for industrial purposes, notably partly manufactured material for the large thread and paper factories in Great Britain. Spruce wood and poplar, for pulp manufacture, exists through the length and breadth of the country to be tapped by the canal system, which can, of course, be handled to much greater advantage by water than by rail. The canal would pass through a country in which all kinds of farm produce can be raised as cheaply, and of as good quality, as in any other country of like latitude, really excelling the most fertile States of the

American Union. A large part of this country is as yet practically undeveloped, owing to lack of transportation facilities. The trade to be drawn through the canal could not but very materially help Ontario and Quebec.

4. If the canal were completed, there is no doubt the cities of Montreal and Quebec would profit greatly thereby. The grain transmitted through the canal from the west would be transhipped to Ocean steamers at Ports on the St. Lawrence, which could not be done without increasing the trade at those points, and the consequent increase in material wealth. The boats would not go back to the west empty but carry in them all kinds of merchandise for those living in the west.

5. Many parts of the territory adjacent to the route of the proposed canal contain immense possibilities for opening up natural deposits of mineral. Forests abound on every hand ; long stretches of farm lands requiring only an outlet in order to be settled upon and cultivated, and splendid water powers capable of producing thousands of horse-power, lying there simply useless, owing to their being off the regular line of traffic and trade. The power to be developed at the Chaudière Rapids in the French River must be immense. A never-ceasing supply of water from Lake Nipissing, with a drop of some 27 feet at the Rapids, should produce enough power to keep in operation a large number of plants, which would have an outlet through the canal.

6. This question is hard for me to answer, involving as it does such large interests. The Ottawa, Arnprior & Parry Sound Company has now secured a fleet of five steamers to run between United States ports and Parry Sound, and will, no doubt, capture some of the trade that has gone formerly through other channels. The canal being a direct waterway from the west to Montreal with but few locks, and a very few miles of canal all told, should be able to give a better rate than *via* the Parry Sound route. If it were not possible to get all the grain down to Montreal in Canal barges from the west before the close of navigation, elevators might be built at North Bay and be filled with grain brought in by larger lake boats, which would be able to find a safe and easy entrance to North Bay *via* the French River and Lake Nipissing. North Bay being much nearer to Montreal than any other lake point on its* line, receiving grain by boat from the west, would be able to get it to Montreal at rates that would compete with existing routes.

7. The construction of the canal would at once advance the lumber and pulp wood industries. Owing to the large bulk of both, in comparison with its value, freight rates have to be, of necessity, much higher than boat rates, owing to the great amount of rolling stock that has to be carried by rail, that is to say, in shipping either by rail the bulk of the freight compared with its value causes very high rates to be charged, while in shipping by water there is no waste room and it can be carried much cheaper on that account. This district through which the canal would pass is heavily wooded, and a large export trade ought to be done in both the products named, by water.

8. Ore can always be handled to better advantage by water than by rail, and therefore the opening up of a water route so much shorter, and with so few natural obstacles in the way of its completion, should give a very material stimulus to the mining and smelting industries of the Ottawa Valley and also of the regions west, which abound in minerals of all kinds.

9. I fancy the rates for transportation of grain from the west to the Atlantic seaboard are now as low as are practicable by the existing routes, and in order to cheapen the cost of getting grain to the Atlantic from the West is to shorten the distance to ocean ports. The northern route, proposed to be utilized in the construction of the canal is at once the shortest and least dangerous route owing to the whole course from the mouth of the French River to Montreal being inland, with the possible exception of Lake Nipissing, on which the waters are sometimes rough, but nothing like what prevails on the large Lakes. Being a safe route and hundreds of miles shorter, the cost of getting grain to the seaboard should be greatly lessened, and will naturally either compel United States routes to do business at a loss or divert the trade this way.

*The Canadian Pacific Railway.

10. The cost of construction should be far less now than in the year 1860. While there was no railway communication in 1860 in the district through which the canal was surveyed, there is now communication by rail with almost every important point, if not all, on the route. Supplies can be brought in anywhere between Montreal and North Bay by rail, within but a few miles of the route, and for the French River Section can be brought in by boat up the French, or across Lake Nipissing from North Bay. The cost of machinery and building material and the facilities for proceeding with such a work are such now that fully 20 per cent deduction ought to be made from estimated cost in 1860.

11. Lake Nipissing is open for navigation just as early as at Sault Ste. Marie or Montreal, in fact, I am of the opinion that we may be a little in advance of both. There having been no statistics kept here, it is hard to give a correct answer, but generally the ice is breaking up and away by the early part of April. After the 15th all is clear. The rivers and other lakes on the route in the neighbourhood of North Bay, are free at the same time. Ice forms about the first of December.

12. No better route could be chosen as a means of military defence.

13. By damming one of the outlets into the French River the waters of Lake Nipissing could be kept at a certain height, fully five feet above the ordinary high water level, without affecting vested interests, except in a very few cases, which would be remedied by the building of dykes at little cost.

Trout Lake could be lowered, on the same principle, by about five feet, making the total drop between the two of, say, fifteen feet. There is a natural channel between the two lakes, almost level, and as far as I have been able to learn, there is no obstacle standing in the way of the feasibility of the scheme, as far as the country surrounding North Bay is concerned.

L. P. SNYDER,
Manager Traders Bank.

NORTH BAY, March 18, 1898.

Mr. Dustan's answers to questions 1, 2, 4 and 12 as requested in your annexed list of questions:

1. By promoting settlement and developing her natural resources it cannot but add immensely to the volume of Canada's trade, both domestic and foreign.

2. The permanent prosperity of the Dominion depends not so much on its gold fields as on the development of the natural products of the great North-west grain-growing and cattle raising area. Ministers of the Crown have expressed their intention of devoting themselves to this object. No better means and no more important factor towards obtaining it can be found than improving the conditions of carriage of these products to their markets, and there can be no fear of overdoing this. A very small reduction in the cost of transportation of wheat will soon increase the production enormously. The time is not far distant when existing routes will be altogether insufficient for carrying the traffic even under present conditions. The Ottawa waterway will not merely share existing traffic, but will create new traffic to an extent that can hardly be over-estimated, and will in itself prove the best colonization measure that could be devised in the interest of the North-west. It will give the people of the North-west a safe, direct and sheltered water route—almost an air line from the Sault to Montreal—greatly reducing both cost and risk of carriage. The St. Lawrence route will always be exposed to severe competition on Lake Erie. By the Ottawa route the traffic will be taken from the Sault and the mouth of Lake Michigan entirely through Canadian waters, and every dollar spent on transportation will remain in Canada. By lessening the cost per bushel of transportation of wheat, it will proportionately increase the profits of farmers in the North-west, and will thus directly and in a large degree aid the material wealth, prosperity and settlement of the North-west.

4. This waterway would be the means of carrying immense quantities of grain to Montreal, which without it will find their way to New York. One of the most serious drawbacks of Montreal as a port is the shortness of the grain shipping season. The opening of the Ottawa route, on which the season will be practically the

same as that at Montreal, will more than double the capacity and opportunity for handling grain at the time when most needed, and must stimulate proportionately the shipping trade of Montreal.

12. Its approaches in both directions are readily defensible. It is far from the frontier and safe from attack and will afford a base of supplies and operations, as well as a means of communication with the Great Lakes, and of shelter for vessels employed in lake commerce.

Very respectfully submitted by,
GEORGE GORDON DUSTAN.

DARTMOUTH, NOVA SCOTIA,
 6th April, 1898.

---

1. There can be no doubt on this point, as it would make available the natural resources of the Ottawa valley, which must otherwise to a large extent remain dormant. This would bring in a large population and start many industries and create a demand for many commodities from other parts of the Dominion. It would also form another great and cheap avenue for commerce, which would be of great advantage to the whole of Canada and to an important part of the United States.

2. It would form a shorter, safer and cheaper route to and from the seaboard than any of the present waterways, and the competition between the carriers by the various routes would be beneficial to the farmers, ranchers, &c., of these parts, whose prosperity depends so largely on the freight rates.

3. Grain would be the largest item, but the following would be very considerable: raw products of the forest, manufactured products of the forest, such as sawn lumber, pulp, &c., mineral products, such as iron, copper, nickle, phosphates, &c., also coal, heavy merchandise for the West and for the locality, farm products from the locality, &c. It would benefit both Provinces.

4. It would do more than anything up to the present time to make Montreal what she should be, one of the largest shipping ports on this Continent, and possibly eventually the largest. It would also benefit Quebec.

5. Most of the products of this locality are of great bulk and weight in proportion to their value, and depend on cheap transportation to make their being worked remunerative. It would also make the immense water powers of the Ottawa available for manufacturing purposes.

6. It would render possible the development of many resources of the locality, which cannot be done by railways, and from which the latter would derive great benefit.

7. It would give great impetus to these industries, and make them more remunerative. This district possesses unrivalled opportunities for the development of the pulp industry. It would also furnish cheap transportation for lumber going East and West.

8. It would render possible the development of these resources which are known to exist in abundance in the Valley, especially as the water powers can be utilized in the treatment of the ores by electricity, &c.

9. It would lower the rates, but to what extent depends largely on the draught of the canal, &c., also on the toll charged for going through. When this canal is built, there is little doubt but that it will be immediately extended to the Hudson, which would largely increase the traffic through both the Montreal-Ottawa and Georgian Bay Canal and those of the St. Lawrence, and Canada must of necessity derive some advantage from this.

10. There would probably be little difference for the same draught of canal—·10 or 12 feet.

11. The season of Navigation at the east end would be the same as at Montreal. In the centre and west end about the same as at Sault Ste. Marie.

12. It would form the only means of water communication with the Upper Lakes and could easily be kept open in case of trouble with the United States, and it might possibly be the means of giving us the command of these waters which would be invaluable to the Dominion.

13. About three years ago I went carefully over Messrs. Walter Shanly and T. C. Clark's reports, estimates, &c., and have traversed a considerable portion of the route, and consider that there are no serious engineering difficulties to be contended with, and that the cost of construction will be found wonderfully small for so important an undertaking, and worthy of the fullest consideration by the Honourable Members of the Senate Committee.

R. ADAMS DAVY.

1. Yes, think it must inevitably do so by giving Montreal a chance to compete successfully with New York as the emporium for the carrying trade of the northern half of the continent.

2. It would give them a shorter and cheaper outlet to the sea and enable Canadian wheat to compete with that of Argentine, India and Southern Europe in markets of the Old World in price as well as quality.

3. The trade done through it would be in the end all the heavier and bulkier exports and imports of the Central, Western, North-western and South-western States of the Union and of Manitoba and the Territories. This would tend to build up Montreal and through Montreal the adjacent Provinces. Independently of this the Ottawa Valley itself is known to be very rich in minerals, lumber and wood pulp material, but these products are too bulky and heavy in proportion to their value to be transported by railway to any great extent. The Ottawa navigation and the numerous branches opening from it would provide a cheaper mode of carriage which would stimulate these industries to an incalculable extent.

4. I have already stated that I believe Montreal and Quebec would soon outstrip New York as the depots for the trade of the Continent. The St. Lawrence and the Great Lakes are the natural outlet to the east, but the great bend southward from Sault St. Marie to Toledo, and the barrier to navigation at Niagara, and the rapids and shoals between Prescott and Montreal have discouraged its being used below Lake Erie, and thence the shortest route to the sea is *via* New York. The re-opening of the old outlet of Lake Huron down the Ottawa Valley would completely change the conditions. A paper by Mr. T. C. Clarke on "The decaying commerce of New York" in Engineering News of 31st March, will be interesting and instructing from this point of view.

5. I have in answer to Question 3 touched upon the local resources of the Ottawa Valley. It is difficult to say to what extent a reduction of freight rates by one-half or two-thirds would affect industries to which railway rates are practically prohibitive. Further than this the navigation works would of themselves render enormous water power now running to waste, available so much so that the whole Ottawa Valley could be supplied with light and electrical power at such rates as would completely discount the use of steam, and make it the most favoured district for manufacturing industry in the world.

6. Anything which affects the general prosperity of a district, and stimulates commercial activity within is a help to the railways in that district. The traffic of the canal would be such as the railways could not carry in any case, and the competition, if any, would be with the American lines terminating in New York and Boston rather than with the Canadian.

The prosperity of the New York Central paralleled for its entire length by the Erie Canal is a case in point.

The Canadian Pacific is in a sense in competition with the St. Lawrence waterway between Fort William and Montreal, but how much traffic would the Canadian Pacific Railway get if this waterway were closed? Would its existence be possible in a commercial sense without it? And how much grain would be grown for export in Manitoba were there no other outlet. The canal will directly and indirectly support an enormous industrial population, which will give business and prosperity to the railways.

7. In this connection I think the word "affect" is hardly appropriate, and that the canal can hardly be spoken of as "affecting" what it would naturally create. The lumber industry has of course existed for nearly a half century, but only as

regards the finer grades, the coarser, of which pulp may be said to be one form are unable commercially speaking to pay the cost of transport under existing circumstances, and the spruce, tamarack, cedar, Norway pine, balsam, ash, birch and poplar of the Ottawa Valley remain practically untouched.

8. The answer to this would be almost the same. That cheap carriage of coal, ore, limestone, &c., and cheap power for electrolytic purposes are conditions without which these industries cannot exist.

9. The paper of Mr. T. C. Clarke, elsewhere referred to, and which is compiled from the opinions and statistics of the most able authorities extant, is a better and more exhaustive answer to this question than I should be justified in giving at the present time. He estimates the cost of carriage of a bushel of grain by the Ottawa navigation and its extension through Lake Champlain to the Hudson from Chicago to New York at 2·07 cents. By the Lake steamers to Buffalo and Erie Canal thence to New York, the cost is put at 5·31 cents. Comment is hardly necessary.

10. Cost of construction of similar works has been reduced by more than one-half, as for instance rock was estimated at $4 per cubic yard, and could now be handled for $1.50 or less. In addition to this newer and more modern methods of construction would be substituted, in many cases resulting in a further saving in construction or maintenance, or both.

11. There is in my opinion no reason why the route should not be available for the same range of dates as that at Sault Ste. Marie, which is virtually the same as the opening and closing at Montreal.

13. So much has been thought out, written and said about the possibilities of this navigation scheme that it is impossible to answer this question at once fully and concisely. The feasibility has been repeatedly reported on by the most distinguished men in the Profession, Walter Shanley, T. C. Clark, Marcus Smith, A. M. Wellington and others. One of the most remarkable points in this connection is that the almost universal presence of hard, solid rock at the salient points, which, in the 60's was looked upon as a drawback, and a source of almost insuperable difficulty, has come to be regarded as one of the happiest conditions. Lock chambers become little more than rock excavations, instead of the great masses of concrete, masonry and puddle seen on other canals. The frowning walls of rock which shut in the Valley of the Upper Ottawa and Mattawa are exactly what we should choose as the material and the foundation and abutments of the dams and controlling works giving miles, not of canal, but of deep slackwater navigation through artificial lakes. And the fact of the existence of the Canadian Pacific Railway and the towns of North Bay, though urged by opponents as an insuperable barrier to the construction of the canal on the original lines involving the raising of the level of Lake Nippissing, has lead to further examination and the resultant discovery that this elevation of the water, so far from being necessary, is inadvisable, and that by retaining the present highwater level we increase the cost very little, decrease the amount of lockage, and completely set at rest any question of the sufficiency of water supply. The railway and the towns become agents which greatly facilitate instead of hindering the construction. On the French River the way in which nature has provided lock-sites, storage, reservoirs, and waste-channels and harbours is more than remarkable.

As to finance there seems no doubt as to the possibilities of the canal being profitable to the promoters, if built by private enterprise alone, but in view of the vast military and political interests involved, it becomes a very grave question whether the State is justified in allowing the work to be constructed altogether by private, and it may be largely by alien, capital. One far-seeing and highly educated man in writing to me from Toledo, uses the expression, "Canada holds the gateway of continental commerce." The editor of *Engineering News* speaks of the canal as being on a route provided by nature through Canadian territory for the carriage of American commerce.

Without quoting others these quotations are very significant. I have myself compiled a map showing that two millions of square miles, mostly south of the line and west of Chicago is largely dependent on it. Would not the control of such a waterway, when built, be an absolute necessity for the Dominion and Imperial

Governments? And would it not be a closer tie between the two Nations on this
continent, with the difference from other similar questions which have arisen before,
that in this case instead of the Dominion being in any degree dependent upon the
United States, a large portion of the latter would soon become dependent almost for
its existence upon the goodwill of the Canadian Government. The canal closed to
their grain immediately causes the latter to drop in value from two to five cents per
bushel, enough to make all the difference between the profit and loss. The same
canal which carries the grain out is capable of carrying apparatus of war in. And
it would almost seem that it is not too much to look forward to a closer political
bond between Canada and the North-western States, not in the form of Annexation
of the former, but rather the voluntary union of the latter with Canada under a
central Government upon the banks of the great waterway itself, which has from our
earliest history been so paramount a factor in the settlement, exploration, commerce
and political division, not only of Canada, but of the major part of the Continent.

HENRY K. WICKSTEED,

Sec. Can. Soc., C. E.

REPORT UPON THE WATER POWER ATTAINABLE FROM THE OTTAWA RIVER WHEN THE MONTREAL, OTTAWA AND GEORGIAN BAY CANAL IS BUILT, BY ANDREW BELL, C.E., OF ALMONTE.

There is probably no river on this Continent from which such a large available
amount of power can be obtained as from the Ottawa. The falls and rapids which
are spread over the distance, from Mattawa eastward, of 300 miles, with a fall in
that distance of over 500 feet, are distributed in such manner that it is possible to
make use of a large percentage of the power.

The flow of water, although subject to considerable variation between high and
low water, is more regular than most rivers on this Continent, on account of the
large number of Lakes on it and its tributaries, and because the Upper waters, that
is above Lake Temiscamingue, are on elevated northern country where the spring
floods are let loose two or three weeks later than in the lower parts of the river.

The volume of the river shows little, if any, apparent diminution from its con-
fluence with the St. Lawrence for 300 miles upwards to Mattawa.

The flow, as measured by me at Carillon, but with only crude appliances, from
1872 to 1882, was ascertained to be. highest water, 12,000,000 cubic feet per minute,
and lowest 1,500,000 per minute. That lowest is the extreme. Average low water
would range from 1,800,000 to 2,000,000 cubic feet per minute.

In constructing the Montreal-Ottawa and Georgian Bay Canal, a large number
of dams must be built to raise the water in most of the reaches, and to concentrate
or localize the water as required at locks, and generally to control the river as
needed for canal purposes, &c. These dams must have the effect of regulating, as
well as increasing, the discharge during low water, as they will retain a portion of
the spring floods for use during the low stages of the river. Besides it may be
advisable, and perhaps necessary, in order to keep up to the required height some of
the reaches, to put storage dams on many of the tributaries. It is safe to say that
this regulating and storage will be done to such an extent that 2,500,000 cubic feet
per minute can be depended upon as the lowest discharge at any time of the year.
This would give (in round numbers) 4,000 horse power per foot fall, or about
2,000,000 horse power from Mattawa eastward on the main stream, not taking into
account the power (estimated at about a quarter of the foregoing, which could be
obtained from the tributaries near to, and before they fall into, the Ottawa—and not
including the immense extra power which might be developed for three months or
more from high water, or even an average stage between high and low.

As to what proportion of the two million horse power can be made available
for industrial purposes, it is somewhat difficult to say. A large quantity will

unavoidably be lost by leakage. Some should be allowed at all seasons to run over the crests of the dams to preserve them, some may be in such a geographical position as not to be easily brought wholly into use, and some will be required to operate the canal. However, it is probable that from 40 to 50 per cent of it may in time be made to do effective work, say at least 800,000 horse power.

The possibilities of such an immense, easily available, power can hardly be overestimated, and besides that there is as well what can be utilized during part year from high water.

ANDREW BELL,
M. Am. Soc. C. E., Consulting Engineer.

SUPPLEMENTARY REPORT BY MR. T. C. CLARKE.

McLeod Stewart, Esq.,
Montreal, Ottawa & Georgian Bay Canal Company, Ottawa, Canada.

Dear Sir,—I have the honour to submit the following Report. bringing down to the present date the matters treated upon in my report of 1860.

Great changes have taken place since that Report demonstrated the feasibility of improving the Ottawa and French Rivers into one of the greatest channels of commerce. What was then only a scientific discussion has now become a matter of great importance to two nations.

Including together the present exports from the basin of the Great Lakes, both in the United States and Canada, there is enough traffic in sight to warrant a large expenditure in opening a new route, if the conditions are such that the cost of transportation between the Lakes and the Ocean can be diminished. Canada alone does not at present furnish enough traffic. The Ottawa route must be treated as an international one.

Two remarkable changes have taken place during the last ten years, which have each resulted in greatly lessening the cost of water transportation; one, upon the Lakes, and the other between the North Atlantic ports of the United States.

The construction of the locks at the outlet of Lake Superior has developed a traffic vast in size, and differing from all others in the world, in that it enables vessels to get full cargoes in both directions during the whole season of open navigation.

The United States lake ports will all be deepened to 20 feet very soon. Steamers now carry cargo of 6,000 tons of grain and iron ore eastward to South Chicago, Cleveland and Buffalo, and take back cargoes of coal to upper Lake ports. It is a well known axiom that the larger the vessel the cheaper it can handle the freight. These 6,000 ton steamers have carried grain from Chicago to Buffalo for $1\frac{36}{100}$ cts. per bushel, which is less than one-half of one mill per ton-mile. Hence there has arisen a popular demand for ship canals of 20 or even 25 feet deep, from the lakes to the ocean. Even if such canals were built and could be used free of tolls, no such economy of transportation by large steamers could take place as in the open lakes.

The rate of speed of thirteen miles an hour would be reduced to five, as in the Suez canal. Canal traffic would not give full cargoes in both directions, and more detention in port would be necessary than at Cleveland or Duluth where whole cargoes of 6,000 tons of coal or ore have been handled by machinery in less than one day. The large steamer is a very expensive machine, and if she were not able to make as many trips per season as she now does, much of her economy would be lost.

It does not now seem possible, except at a prohibitory cost, to deepen the Ottawa navigation to 20 feet, and fortunately it is not necessary.

The second change, which has resulted in lessening the cost of transportation between Atlantic ports, suggests the true method of improving the Ottawa.

Some ten years since all coal was carried between the shipping ports of Philadelphia and New York to other Atlantic ports, chiefly those of New England, in single collier steamers, at a cost of $1.50 to $1.75 per ton.

Now it is carried in tows of three or four large barges drawing from 16 to 18 feet of water, towed by a single powerful tug boat. This tug does not wait in port for coal to be loaded or unloaded, but each tug has many barges, and she picks up her tow of full or empty barges without detention, as a locomotive does cars. In this way many trips are made per season. The distance between Philadelphia and Boston and return is about 800 miles, and coal is now carried for an average of 75 cents per ton, which is nine-tenths of a mill per ton-mile.

This economy of transportation has increased the coal traffic to some twenty-five millions of tons annually, which is as great as the tonnage annually passing through the Detroit River. The use of these tows of barges is fast increasing upon the upper lakes.

All these facts have been clearly set forth by Major T. W. Symons, United States Engineer Corps, in his admirable and exhaustive report to the United States Congress in 1897. He shows that if the Erie Canal were deepened to 11 feet and grain were carried in tows of barges of 1,500 tons capacity, it could be carried from Chicago to New York, including reasonable transhipment charges at Buffalo from large steamers into canal boats, for less than steamers of 20 feet draft could carry it through the Erie Canal if that could possibly be deepened to over 20 feet, and steamers run continuously from Chicago to New York. In both cases tolls are not taken into account.

The estimated cost of the 11 foot canal is fifty million dollars, and of the 20 foot 200 millions.

The great value of the Ottawa navigation is this: Out of the 975 miles between Chicago and Montreal 591 miles is an inland or perfectly protected navigation, leaving but 384 miles of open lake. In open lake a speed of 4½ miles an hour can be made by tows of barges. In the protected portion an average speed of ten miles an hour can be made. The cost of insurance by this route would be much less than by any other.

By the Welland and St. Lawrence route, there are 991 miles of open lake navigation, and but 297 of inland or protected navigation. The depth of the Welland and St. Lawrence Canals would limit the draft of barges to 13½ feet, which is too shallow for navigation in lakes such as Erie, subject to sudden violent storms. The rates of insurance would be greater, and the longer time required, owing to greater length, and slower movement through the unprotected parts, would more than make up for the 22 days of longer open navigation by the Welland route.

I recommend that the scale of the Ottawa navigation be fixed as follows:— Locks 300 feet long x 45 feet wide x 14 feet deep, capable of passing steel barges 280 feet long, 42 foot beam and carrying 3,100 tons net on 13½ feet draft water.

The excavated channels should be fifteen feet deep and have five times the area of the vessel, with sufficient room for two vessels to pass each other, which would give a width of 160 feet on the bottom and 170 feet at low water level.

The cost of carrying grain from one of the lake ports, say Chicago, to Montreal by the Ottawa route, would be as follows :—

CAPACITY.

A tow would consist of three steel barges, each 280 x 42 x 20 feet, moulded depth, carrying, on 13½ feet draft, 3,100 net tons. These would be towed by a powerful tug steamer capable of towing the barges at the rate of four and one-half miles per hour in open lake, and ten miles per hour through the sheltered lakes and rivers of the Ottawa navigation. The tug steamer would be capable of carrying a cargo of 1,200 tons, making a total capacity of 10,500 tons.

TIME.

Open lake—
Chicago to a point near the mouth of St. Mary's river—380 miles at 4½ miles per hour.. 72·2 hours.

Inland lakes and rivers—
St. Mary's River to French River, 160 miles
Ottawa navigation................ 401   "

	561 " at 10..	56·1 hours.
Canals................... .. ..,	29·3 miles at 2·9	10· hours.

Lockages 1½ minutes per foot

for each vessel $\dfrac{1\frac{1}{2} \times 4 = 6 \times 682 \text{ ft.}}{60 \text{ min.}}$ .... 68·2 hours.

Total.. .... 206·5 hours.

206·5 x 2 = 413 hours.
In port   91 hours.

504 hours, or 21 days round trip.

The open season of navigation on this route, is limited by the closing of Lake Nipissing and gives an open season of 213 days, or ten round trips.

COST.

1 tug....................	$125,000
4 barges (1 extra) at $75,00	300,000

	$425,000 interest and depreciation at 5 per cent....................	$21,250
Insurance on hulls, 2 per cent.......		8,500
" on cargo		
Going East 10 x 10,500......	105,000 Tons.	
" West ⅓	35,000 "	
	140,000 Tons at $20.	
	$2,800,000 at 25c. per 100......	7,000
Expenses of tug—full subsistence, wages and small repairs, $100 per day for 213 days.............		21,300
4 barges at $7.50 per day—30 x 213....		6,390
Profits 10 per cent....		6,440
		$70,880

which divided by 140,000 Tons gives as the cost about 50c. per ton, or 1½ cts. per bushel.

It is absolutely essential to the success of this project that there should be ample elevator facilities at the port of Montreal, so that Ocean steamers should suffer no detention. With such an elevator of the capacity of one million bushels as lately has been built by the Great Northern Railway at Buffalo, the whole cost of elevating and storage should not exceed three quarters of a cent, making the total cost per bushel 2¼ cents, which is far below the cost by any existing route, or than can be obtained on the Welland and St. Lawrence route when the canals are completed.

This extremely low cost is based on the assumption of full cargoes going east, and one-third full going west. The larger the amount of business done, the more nearly will this be realized, and the financial success of the scheme would be enhanced, if the Ottawa navigation could be extended upon the same scale, through Lake Champlain to New York, the feasibility of which the United States Deep Water Ways Commission are now, it is believed, investigating. By this route the distance from Chicago to New York, would be about 1,353 miles, of which 380 miles would be open lakes, 847 miles inland navigation, and 126 miles of canals.

By similar calculations to those above given, eight trips could be made in an open season of 235 days, and the cost would be 2 cents per bushel, to which should be added the present elevator and other charges at the port of New York, which are very high, amounting to $1\frac{1}{2}$ cents per bushel, or a total of $3\frac{1}{2}$ cents per bushel. Major Symons estimates that when the Erie Canal is deepened to 9 feet and the locks lengthened, wheat can be carried from Chicago to New York for 3·67 cents to which add New York, terminal charge 1·50 cents a total of 5·17 cents; showing the superiority of the Ottawa route.

The cost of interest, maintenance and repairs, lock tending, electric lighting, etc., on the Ottawa route, would be borne by moderate tolls and leases of water power, described hereafter.

As compared with the estimated cost of the Ottawa navigation in 1860, there will be an increase of quantities and a diminution of cost in item prices.

The increase of the size of the locks from 250 x 45 x 12 to 300 x 45 x 14, will increase quantities. Also the enlargement of the prism of the excavated canal from 146 x 13 to 160 x 15, will increase quantities.

The locks at Grenville and Carillon will have to be enlarged. The Lachine locks will also have to be lengthened unless it is decided not to use the present crowded Lachine Canal, and improve one of the branches of the Ottawa north of the Island of Montreal.

Another increase of cost is due to the fact that Lake Nipissing cannot now be raised by damming its outlets, as was proposed in 1860.

The country around the summit lakes is now well settled and has many cultivated farms. The town of North Bay, which would have to be moved back to prevent overflow, has some 2,500 inhabitants. Thirty miles of the Canadian Pacific Railway would have to be moved or raised.

The level of Lake Nipissing must still be maintained from French River to the Mattawan, 57 miles. This means lowering the level of Trout and Turtle Lakes to coincide with that of Nipissing, which can be done. This is the only way in which sufficient water for lockages can be obtained. The total lockage will be reduced from 715 to 682 feet.

The amount of excavation will be increased, but it is believed that the extra cost of this will not exceed what would have to be paid for damages if Lake Nipissing were raised.

The plan of 1860, which raised existing levels by dams on the French and Mattawan Rivers and on the Ottawa as far east as Chats Lake, can still be followed, as the shores are steep and rocky, and but little land will be overflowed. There are a few places where sites of locks and dams may have to be changed, but not at an increased cost.

In 1860 the whole Upper Ottawa was a wilderness. All materials and supplies above Deep River must then have been transported partly by teams and partly in batteaux towed by horses, or poled by men. Now, the Canadian Pacific Railway can deliver materials, supplies and men all along the route, and at far less cost.

Several locks of low lift can now be concentrated into one, as in accordance with the best modern practice. This will reduce cost.

I am in favour of locating the locks so that a duplicate lock can be built hereafter alongside of the one first to be built.

I now advise constructing the locks of concrete (made from the stone near by) and Portland cement. The lock walls can be protected by waling pieces of steel and oak, thus saving much costly cut stone masonry.

The most important item of economy comes from the fact that the cost of the rock excavation, which is the largest item of cost, can be greatly reduced by the improvements which have been made during the past few years in the use of power drills, high explosives, and better kinds of machinery for handling materials.

The air compressors and other machinery can in many cases be driven by electric power derived from the river. The latest price paid for rock excavation on the Chicago Drainage Canal was 59 cents per cubic yard, while the average price estimated for the Ottawa improvements in 1860 was generally from $1.50 to $2.00 per yard.

I am not now prepared to revise the figures of cost made in 1860, as this cannot be done without further examinations and surveys which will take several months to properly carry out.

There are several very important economies in construction that can now be made available, which could not in 1860.

It is proper to point out that the most important change in the situation since 1860 has come from the development of electrical transmission of power. The dams which were designed by me in 1860 were then, and are now, absolutely necessary to give sufficient depth for navigation. These dams will also be the means of developing and controlling water power for electric appliances.

I can state unreservedly that I know of no other place in any manufacturing country, Niagara Falls not excepted, where there is such an amount of water power as this scheme can make available, both for manufacturing purposes and possibly for moving vessels rapidly through the locks.

It is proposed to construct 20 dams on the Ottawa with an average of 20 feet fall each. The low water discharge of the Ottawa never falls below 1,500,000 cubic feet per minute, of which one third should be allowed to run over the crests of the dams to prevent decay, leaving 1,000,000 cubic feet per minute to run through flumes and do effective work. By the usual formula

Dams cu. ft. per min. fall.

$$\frac{20 \times 1,000,000 \times 62\frac{1}{2} \text{ lbs.} \times 20}{44,000.} \quad \text{we have } 566,360 \text{ horse power.}$$

Adding that available on the Mattawan and French Rivers there will probably be, at a minimum, not less than 700,000 horse power.

The average discharge of the weirs would give not less than four time this amount.

All this can be made available, by the comparatively small expenditure necessary for flumes and the foundations of penstocks and turbines. The cost of the installation of electric plant would vary greatly with the situation.

All of which is respectfully submitted by,

THOMAS C. CLARKE,
Consulting Engineer Montreal,
Ottawa and Georgian Bay Navigation.
Member Institution of Civil Engineers
and of the American Society of
Civil Engineers.

NEW YORK, 16th February, 1898.

EXTRACTS FROM PROSPECTUS OF THE MONTREAL, OTTAWA AND GEORGIAN BAY CANAL COMPANY GIVING DISTANCES.

The opening up of the Ottawa route would complete a direct and unbroken navigation along the continuation of such line for 2,000 miles into the heart of the Western continent, and would thus form an important link in the greatest of international waterways.

2. Owing to its directness this route effects a saving in distance between western lake ports and ocean navigation of almost 450 miles over the Erie, and 375 over the St. Lawrence. Thus from Chicago to Montreal is

Via the St. Lawrence...1,348 miles
" Ottawa.. 980 "

378 "

While from Chicago to

      New York via the Erie route is..............................1,415 miles
      Montreal via the Ottawa.............   980   "

                                                  435   "

    It is 575 miles from the entrance of Lake Michigan to Buffalo (which port of transhipment is 495 miles miles from an ocean port), while the total distance from the same point of departure to the head of ocean navigation at Montreal via the Ottawa is only 635 miles. In other words, a vessel leaving Chicago would reach the Atlantic market at Montreal in fifty or sixty miles more than it now takes her to reach Buffalo.

    The distances between Chicago and Liverpool by the several routes are as follows :—

    1. Via Erie Canal,

           Chicago to Buffalo........... .... 920 miles.
           Erie Canal to Albany. 350   "
           Hudson River to New York....................... 145   "
           New York to Liverpool 3,080   "

                                             4,195   "

    2. Via the St. Lawrence,

           Chicago to Montreal....... ....,............ 1,348 miles.
           Montreal to Liverpool.............. .., ... 2,800   "

                                             4,148   "

    3. Via the Ottawa,

           Chicago to Montreal .... 980 miles.
           Montreal to Liverpool............ 2,800   "

                                           3,780   "

or over 700 miles less via the Ottawa route than by way of the Erie.

    3. Less canalling is required on the Ottawa route than on any other. According to the plan submitted by Mr. T. C. Clarke, C.E., only 29 miles of canal are necessary on this route as against 71 on the St. Lawrence and 351 on the Erie. Estimating one mile of canal navigation as equivalent in point of expense and delay involved to three miles of open river and lake navigation, the routes will compare as follows: —

    From Chicago to Atlantic tide water, via

1. Ottawa route, 980 miles (951+(29×3)=   87) equivalent to 1,038 ⎫ miles of
2. St. Lawrence 1,348   " (1,277+(71×3)= 213)   "   1,490 ⎬ open river
3. Erie,   1,415   " (1,064+(351×3)=1,053)   "   2,117 ⎭ and lake navigation.

    4 Calculating the average rate of travel at four miles per hour for canal and twelve miles for open river and lake, the time consumed on the several trips will be (allowing for lockage at the rate of 1½ minutes per foot).

    1. Via Erie to New York,

	Miles.	Hrs.	Mins.
Lake and River.........	1,064	88	40
Canal......................	351 (655 ft. lockage)	104	05
Total..........		192	45

2. Via St. Lawrence to Montreal,

	Miles.		Hrs.	Mins.
Lake and River.......	1,277		106	25
Canal.	71	(553 ft. lockage)	31	35
Total......................................			138	...

Via Ottawa to Montreal,

	Miles.		Hrs.	Mins.
Lake and River..... ...	951		79	15
Canal.....................	29	(666 ft. lockage)	23	55
Total.. .. ..,.....,.....			103	10

showing a saving of nearly four days over the Erie route, and one and one-half days over the St. Lawrence.

www.ingramcontent.com/pod-product-compliance
Lightning Source LLC
Chambersburg PA
CBHW032121080426
42733CB00008B/1013